Beautiful
Britain

Beautiful
Britain

Bernard Miles

Edited by Keith Lye B.A., F.R.G.S.

Hamlyn

Dedication

I was naturally very happy to be writing a book about Beautiful Britain, but when I came to examine my qualifications, I began to realize how little I knew about some of the truly basic facts, viz. How did it get there? What was it made of? What was it sitting on? How and why was it changing its shape from year to year? And so on.

It was clear I should need a tutor, someone who could fill me in on all these vital matters. And I was lucky to meet Keith Lye, a geographer, an accomplished writer and a born teacher, with a highly developed sense of humour, who was willing to give me tutorials, mark my homework (he once gave me a beta minus!) and generally act as my guide and supervisor. It is to him, therefore, that I venture to dedicate the following pages.

Photographic acknowledgements
British Tourist Authority, London, pages 71, 114–115; W. F. Davidson, Cumbria, pages 26, 46–47 top, 69, 70, 76–77, 78, 80 bottom, 96–97, 100, 102, 103, 105, 106, 112, 115, 116, 120 bottom, 112, 123 top, 129, 144 bottom, 148, 149, 150–151, 152, 160 top, 167, 188 top, 194, 196 bottom, 202 bottom, 206, 207, 208, 209, 210, 216, 220, 227 bottom, 228 bottom, 230, 231, 235, 236–237; Carlos Faulds, London, pages 190–191, 192–193, 213; Fotobank International Colour Library, London, pages 18, 31, 32, 33, 42–43 top, 45, 46–47 bottom, 58, 62, 64, 73, 74, 75 top, 80 top, 83, 84, 85 bottom, 87 bottom, 88–89, 90, 91, 94, 95, 107, 113, 114, 118–119, 125, 130, 132, 133, 134, 135, 242 top, 243, 245, 250 top; John Green, London, pages 159, 161 bottom, 183; Michael Holford, London, pages 7, 10, 48–49 bottom, 51, 52–53, 56–57, 60–61, 63, 72, 82, 142, 143 bottom, 145, 164–165, 171, 173 top, 180 top, 181 top, 200–201, 202 top, 204–205, 216–217, 218–219; Susan Lund, Buckinghamshire, pages 8, 37, 42–43 bottom, 48 top, 49 top, 50, 104, 215, 229, 232, 233; Spectrum Colour Library, London, pages 16, 38–39, 54, 55, 152–153, 162–163, 180–181, 211, 214 top, 251; Judy Todd, London, pages 27 top, 68–69, 146, 151, 176 bottom, 179, 188 bottom, 249 bottom, 250 bottom; Rex Wailes, Buckinghamshire, page 67; ZEFA, London, pages 9, 11, 13, 14–15, 19, 20–21, 22, 23, 24, 25, 27 bottom, 28, 29, 30, 34, 35, 36, 40, 42, 44, 47, 64–65, 66, 74–75 bottom, 81, 85 top, 86, 87 top, 92–93, 98, 101, 108, 109, 110, 111, 120 top, 123 bottom, 124, 126, 127, 128–129, 131, 136–137, 138, 140, 141, 143 top, 144 top, 147, 154–155, 156, 158, 160 bottom, 161 top, 166–167, 168, 169, 170, 172, 173 bottom, 174–175, 176 top, 178, 182–183, 184, 185, 186–187, 190, 194–195, 196 top, 197, 198, 199, 212, 214 bottom, 221, 222–223, 224, 226, 227 top, 228 top, 234–235, 236, 238–239, 240, 242 bottom, 244, 246, 247, 248, 249 top, 252.

Front cover:	Durham Cathedral (Tony Stone Associates)
Back cover:	Near Penrith, Cumbria (Tony Stone Associates)
Endpapers (front):	Bickleigh, Devon (Tony Stone Associates)
(back):	Ullapool Pier, Ross and Cromarty, Scotland (Tony Stone Associates)
Title spread:	Wharfedale, Yorkshire (Tony Stone Associates)

Published by Hamlyn Publishing
Astronaut House, Feltham, Middlesex, England

Prepared by Deans International Publishing
52–54 Southwark Street, London SE1 1UA
A division of The Hamlyn Publishing Group Limited
London · New York · Sydney · Toronto

Copyright © The Hamlyn Publishing Group Limited 1984
ISBN 0 600 34789 3

Printed and bound by Graficromo s.a., Cordoba, Spain

Contents

Preface

'If God tries to prepare for me a Heaven more beautiful than I enjoy here, He will fail,' said the German lady sitting on my right. We were dining with a clergyman friend and his family in their vicarage home overlooking Lake Windermere, and talk had turned upon matters of life and death and what to expect in the Hereafter. 'Your great poet Wordsworth wrote that "Heaven lies about us in our infancy", but I am 53 years old and I feel it lying about me here and now. I am a fugitive from Hitler, with an adoring husband and three fine children. I live in a simple stone farmhouse in this heavenly landscape and I feel I am enchanted. Every moment of the day I pray that the spell may not be broken. What more could God do for me?'

Our host, shepherd of his local flock, laughed good-humouredly. 'That's a question you'll find hard to answer,' he said. But it set me thinking that the challenge thrown down by our friend might form the substance of a book, a first shot at trying to prove whether the good lady was right or wrong. So here goes! What is Britain? How did it come about? What are its characteristics? What makes it different from other lands and what right have we to call it 'a glimpse of Heaven on Earth?' How was it born? How did it grow from swaddling clothes to adulthood?

About 10,000 years ago Britain was part of the single land mass which we know as Europe. But all those centuries ago the waters began to rise and the sea invaded the tongue of land between our island home and the land to its east, cutting us off from Europe and creating, where there had once been a solid causeway, a wide, protective moat – the Strait of Dover. This great event, completed about 7,500 years ago, set us free to breathe the first faint whisper of that precious and jealously guarded phrase: 'An Englishman's home is his castle.' And that is where our story begins.

Britain was a separate group of islands, free to develop its own characteristics, free to adopt other countries' word forms, free to invent its own patterns of agriculture and architecture, and free to invent its own special life-style. Already a 'precious stone set in a silver sea', Britain would be chiselled and polished by the oncoming centuries, its hundreds of facets each reflecting back a different fragment of its development: the battle to tame the primeval forest; breaking the soil with plough and harrow; sowing and reaping; the long progress from cave dwellings to such man-made shelters as Skara Brae (a housing estate of ancient people); on to the wheel and the windmill, the fishhook, fire and furnace for cooking and

7

smelting; and the invention of rope with its endless range of knots and bends (what genius invented the bowline and its running sister?). And so on to the mastery of building techniques, either invented or borrowed, as seen in the apse and the arch, but all executed in Britain with subtle and recognizable variations. Even vessels working the waters around the coast have their own peculiar characteristics. We may have begun with dugout canoes and coracles, but today we have a score or more of craft, each one built to suit a peculiar shoreline and the tides and currents which vex it – the Sussex ketch, the Mersey flat, the Severn trow, the Humber keel, the Norfolk wherry, the Thames bawley, the Mumbles skiff, the Penzance lugger, the Yorkshire coble, the Suffolk yawl, the Morecambe shrimper, and so on.

On and on from muttering and grunting and howling, signals of love, hope, surprise and danger, anger and sorrow, gathering on the way the elements of language and grammar, to the Lindisfarne Gospels, Geoffrey Chaucer, Will Shakespeare, John Milton, Sam Johnson, Jane Austen, John Keats, Percy Shelley, Charles Dickens, Thomas Hardy, Gerard Manley Hopkins, W H Auden and Dylan Thomas – what a process, what a progress. But did we do it all by ourselves? Could we have managed without help, without the injection of outside blood and brains?

Once Britain became a fortress guarded by a moat, people on the mainland became envious, and curious to know how things were going here. Raiders bent on conquest and traders eager for commerce paid us many a visit. But the first people to attempt an organized invasion were the Romans under Julius Caesar, first in 55 BC, then in the following year. Caesar had conquered most of France, or Gaul as it was then called. But as he drew near its north-western corner, he found its armies being reinforced by British infantry and cavalry. So he made two powerful raids on Britain to show the natives what they would be up against if they dared to take on the might of Rome.

Nearly 90 years later, the Emperor Claudius attempted a total conquest, but succeeded only in the central, south-eastern and southern parts, leaving rocky Cornwall, mountainous Wales and the ferocious Scots more or less alone. Indeed the only way the Romans could hold the Scots in check was by building a pair of walls from east to west, right the way across the North Country. The Romans ruled Britain for more than 300 years, building townships and roads, planting farms and

A stone circle at Castlerigg, near Keswick, is an ancient but man-made contribution to the Lake District National Park, one of beautiful Britain's crowning glories.

estates, installing baths and central heating. Always the barbarian Picts and Scots were trying to invade from the north, to taste the luxuries of civilized life, shelter from the biting cold, cooked food and the delicious liquid pressed from Italian grapes. Their own rough whisky was good, but the contents of the odd wineskin left behind in one of the captured storehouses – that was different! Many a Scot must have dreamed, long before Keats:

> 'Oh for a beaker full of the warm South,
> Full of the true, the blushful Hippocrene
> With beaded bubbles winking at the brim
> And purple stained mouth!'

And which of us, barbarians to a man, would not agree?

But Rome then fell, to other wild tribes on her northern and eastern flanks – Huns, Vandals and Lombards. The legions which had protected Britain were called home, leaving us naked to the Saxon and Viking raiders from the Frisian coast, Denmark, Norway and Sweden. We know all too little about these people, for they had not learned to write and they built in timber which, over the years, burned down or rotted away. We know that they were heathen, worshipping primitive gods of earth and air, of thunder and lightning, of birth and death, and that they had a ramshackle system of justice (for example, if you could walk across a bed of red-hot nails or hold your hand in a pot of boiling water without getting burned, you were innocent; if not, guilty). But they had a fine sense of ornament and, in the case of the Vikings, had developed one of the finest and most beautiful warboats ever built: the straked longship, 59–69 feet (15–21 metres) from stern to stem, sharp at both ends and of shallow draught, rowed by 30 or 40 oarsmen, with a single square sail to supplement mere

Loch Leven, a deep sea inlet in the south-western corner of Scotland's Highland region, leads to some of Britain's most rugged yet majestic landscapes.

muscle power. These were the people who, under their leader Leif Ericson, got to America more than 400 years before Columbus. So the trip to the gently shelving coast of Britain to seize York and build there as fine a city as any in Norway or Sweden, and then to sail around the Shetlands to Ireland and plant a powerful settlement in Dublin, gave them little trouble.

The Saxons and Vikings came in fury but remained as settlers. The northern counties of Britain are rich with Scandinavian words, but the greatest gifts the Norseman gave us were a fierce independence after more than a quarter of a millennium under the Roman eagle's wings, a love of settlement and home life, a fine taste in ornament and, most important of all, the roots of our unique seafaring heritage which has never withered. One of our dearest pastimes is 'messing about in boats', from Sir Francis Drake and Lord Nelson to the British Navy's battle with the *Scharnhorst* off the North Cape of Norway in 1943 – the last action between two heavy warships, fought in almost total darkness. This was the end of an era and also an end to the hopes of Hitler, the last of our would-be invaders. Except, that is, for an earlier and more benign one which I came near to omitting – Christianity.

Jesus, who offered humanity freedom from the torment of life on Earth and the sure hope of joining Him and His Father in the Life Beyond, had been crucified with the words 'Father, forgive them for they know not what they do' on his lips. This notion of forgiveness and salvation uttered with such certainty and pursued with such burning zeal by His disciples took root and gradually began to break the back of the old pseudo-Greek pantheon of Roman gods until it became at last the established religion in many parts of the world. Thus there came into being the vast structure of the Church Militant and its obedience to the command: 'Go ye into all the world and preach the Gospel.'

Augustine and his team of missionaries landed in Kent in AD 597, set up their headquarters in Canterbury and got to work. They had arrived in a land almost totally heathen and entering one of the darkest periods in its history, so it was a long and uphill struggle. Not until 260 years later, with King Alfred's victory over the Danes and the conversion of their leader Guthrum, could it be said that the tide had really turned. Even so, there were many battles, setbacks, hangings, burnings and beheadings. But Christianity finally captured the whole of Europe, and in England it led to the whole range of exquisite church building which continued for the next 600 to 700 years. Just as civil wars and threats of invasion had developed the art of castle building, so the introduction of Christianity played a crucial role in British architecture and in lifting the British up the ladder of tolerance and humanity. 'I am my brother's keeper' became marginally more than an empty figure of speech.

Why do I tell you all this? Because a country is created by the people who dwell in it, and the people who dwell in it are created by the country. The people and the land they inhabit are inseparable. Landscape is living history, and history is recorded in language.

Only during the last 150 years, when travel has become comparatively cheap and easy, have we achieved a broader mix of blood, becoming the home of millions of refugees from foreign lands and of foreign wives brought home by our servicemen. And the mix is still going on. In fact we are still largely tribal – a Cornishman would find it almost impossible to carry on a conversation with a Geordie. In the 19th century each county (and often separate areas of one county) published glossaries of local words – Yorkshire, Essex, Geordie, Suffolk, Devonshire, Cornish, and so on; they were all so proud of their linguistic identities. You can find all these books in university libraries, along with folk tales and songs. Besides, the earth itself, the land in which villages and farms are planted and from which homes, barns, churches and cathedrals are built, is immensely varied, of many ages, natures and textures: granite, basalt, limestone, chalk, clay, sandstone, shale, flint and slate. And all over the country the forms and names of tools differ, including the names and shapes of wheeled vehicles. A Lincolnshire wagon would be useless in Shropshire; a Berkshire tumbril useless in Dorset. The ruts in the lanes, all of varying widths, would tear them to pieces.

Over the centuries the British have become a unique mix of personality, language, habit, technique and general life-style. If it so happens you are a native of Britain, that is why you are sitting in your armchair with this book on your lap, absorbing your own character, your own identity, expressed by the landscape and the human handiwork that defines it, and by your forefathers who fashioned both, and who were ready to die for them. This book is a pictorial biography. It is about you.

The Ardmore Round Tower in County Waterford is one of a hundred or so in Ireland. Built near churches and monastic sites, they were places of refuge during Viking raids.

Beachy Head is a mass of pure chalk at the eastern end of the South Downs, which extended to the continent until, some 10,000 years ago, the last Ice Age ended and the melted waters gradually flooded the depression between Britain and Europe, creating the English Channel and the splendid isolation which made Britain a nation of seafarers. Back in the early 1900s, my grandfather used to sing: 'Oh, what a right little island, A right little, tight little island. All the world round, No place is found, So happy as this little island!' The isolation has disappeared with the coming of the aeroplane, but the British character had already been moulded – freedom-loving, independent and moderately rational.

South-Eastern England

When, after a long absence abroad, British people catch sight of the white cliffs of Dover, heartbeats quicken and eyes fill with tears. This is home.

The Strait of Dover, which finally cut England off from mainland Europe in about 5500 BC, is the shortest sea route to France, and for at least 3,000 years the French wanted to recapture what was once theirs. For all of these years, and perhaps longer, Dover was a fortress. There was first an Iron Age fort, and in later centuries Roman, Saxon and Norman fortifications. Lastly a fine medieval castle was built by King Henry II and his son King John, a monument now preserved for all time. The need to defend the Kent coast against European transgressors is recalled a little farther south-west, around Lydd and Dungeness, in the strange Martello towers built in the late 18th century to repel Napoleon's forces. It is said that if Hitler had won the war, he intended to divide his time in Britain between Dover Castle and the superb Tudor mansion at Knole, near Sevenoaks, the historic home of the Sackville family.

The white cliffs of Dover mark the eastern extremity of Kent's North Downs, whose rolling chalk country is now preserved in an Area of Outstanding Natural Beauty, as are the similar South Downs of East and West Sussex lower down. Along the North Downs went the pilgrims immortalized in Geoffrey Chaucer's *Canterbury Tales* (c 1387). 'When April comes with its soft showers,' he wrote, 'then people long to go on pilgrimage, the holy blissful martyr for to seek.' The martyr was Archbishop Thomas à Becket, who was murdered in 1170 for defying the king, and it was at his tomb that the pilgrims came to worship. The stone steps leading up to the tomb and the rectangle of marble around the tomb itself are deeply hollowed by the knees of millions of Christians who have

Dover Castle, perched on the hill in the background of this picture, has long given early warning of invaders, including bomber formations from the continent in the Second World War. In Roman times, when Dover was called Dubris, there was a lighthouse here which is still preserved inside the castle. Dover is now a busy port and the starting or finishing point for cross-Channel swimmers, Cap Griz-Nez serving the same function in France. The first man to swim the Channel was Captain Webb, who took 21 hours and 45 minutes to do it back in 1875. But dozens have done so since, including many boys and girls. Indeed, in 1982, a 15-year-old Canadian girl, Cynthia (Cindy) Nicholas swam it both ways in only 18 hours and 55 minutes.

prayed there and offered their thanks for St Thomas's inspiring life. Canterbury is now the mother cathedral of the Church of England, seat of the Archbishop whose solemn duty it is to crown our kings and queens.

South-west of Dover in East Sussex is the charming fishing town of Hastings where my wife and I lived when I was painting scenery and playing small parts on the St Leonard's Palace Pier a short distance away. Off the Hastings coast lies the Dutch ship *Amsterdam*, wrecked there in 1748 with all her cargo and crew. At low tide you can see parts of her oaken ribs sticking up out of the sand. Divers have stolen some of her treasure, but much

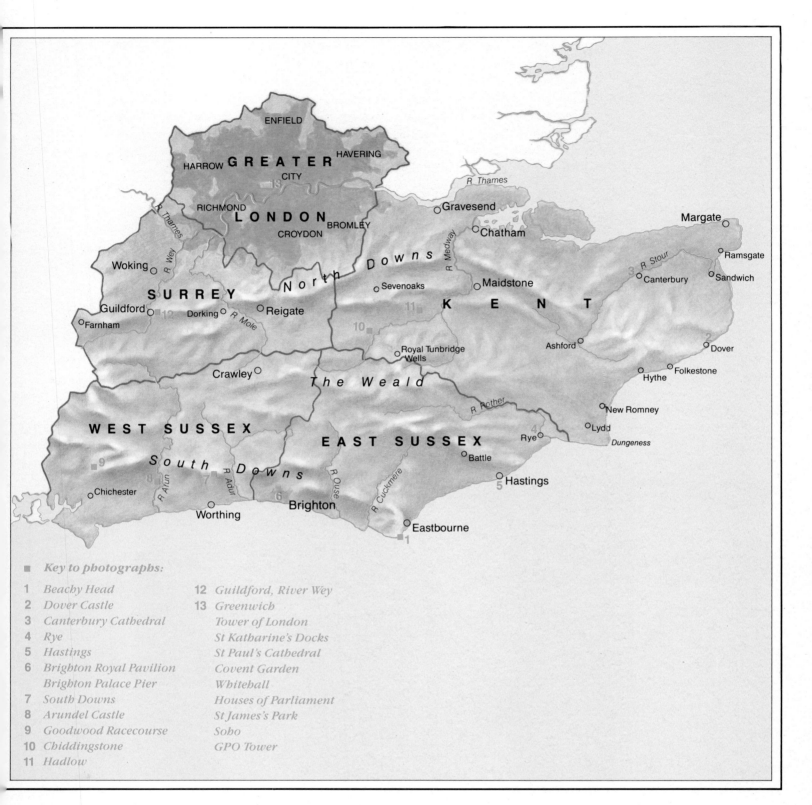

ENFIELD
GREATER HAVERING
HARROW CITY
RICHMOND **LONDON** BROMLEY
CROYDON
R Thames
Gravesend
Chatham
Margate
Ramsgate
R Stour
Woking *North* *Downs* Canterbury Sandwich
SURREY Sevenoaks Maidstone **K E N T**
Guildford Dorking R Mole Reigate
Farnham Ashford Dover
Royal Tunbridge Wells Hythe Folkestone
Crawley New Romney
The *Weald* Lydd
R Rother Dungeness
WEST SUSSEX **EAST SUSSEX** Rye
South *Downs* Battle
R Arun R Adur R Ouse R Cuckmere Hastings
Chichester
Worthing Brighton
Eastbourne

Key to photographs:

1	*Beachy Head*	12	*Guildford, River Wey*
2	*Dover Castle*	13	*Greenwich*
3	*Canterbury Cathedral*		*Tower of London*
4	*Rye*		*St Katharine's Docks*
5	*Hastings*		*St Paul's Cathedral*
6	*Brighton Royal Pavilion*		*Covent Garden*
	Brighton Palace Pier		*Whitehall*
7	*South Downs*		*Houses of Parliament*
8	*Arundel Castle*		*St James's Park*
9	*Goodwood Racecourse*		*Soho*
10	*Chiddingstone*		*GPO Tower*
11	*Hadlow*		

remains to be recovered. Hastings is one of the original Cinque Ports, which faced France and were points of defence against possible invasion. The others were Dover, Hythe, Sandwich and Romney.

North of Hastings is the village of Battle with its abbey commemorating the Battle of Hastings (1066), when William the Conqueror, Duke of Normandy, beat the Saxon King Harold in a long and bloody battle. William was a strong and ruthless ruler, but despite his many cruelties, his reign from 1066 to 1087 gave England a great leap forward in matters of order and organization, having a similar effect to that of the Romans. Indeed, the

17

Hastings in East Sussex was one of the famous Cinque ports (Cinque being French for five) which guarded the vulnerable south-eastern corner of England. One of the most impressive features on the beach at Hastings are the net houses, tall, timber structures in which local fisherman dried and repaired their tackle, ready for the next trip. Just off the coast at low water you can see the ribs of a Dutch merchantman, The Amsterdam, wrecked with all hands in 1748. Archaeologists hope one day to raise her just as the Mary Rose has been raised. And as The Amsterdam is younger than the Mary Rose, she will surely provide much valuable information about seafaring life some 250 years later.

Normans introduced into our land a new style of architecture called, elsewhere in Europe, Romanesque, which included the semi-circular Roman arch, also a quite new concept of scale and weight, and a whole range of new decoration. Like the people who built them, Norman buildings are massive and powerful.

South of Hastings, at Beachy Head, the Sussex coast turns westward towards Brighton, one of England's most celebrated resorts, which is famous for its exquisite Royal Pavilion, a sort of 'stately pleasure dome' in the Indian style, specially designed for the Prince Regent in the early 19th century and filled with priceless furniture and china.

Brighton's Royal Pavilion, planned by George IV and executed by the architect John Nash, comes as a welcome shock to the stolid and self-satisfied British who tend to believe that Romanesque, Gothic, Tudor, Regency, Palladian and high-rise concrete are the be-all and end-all of architecture. But here are onion-shaped domes and attendant pinnacles not rivalling, but certainly reminiscent of, the Taj Mahal. The Pavilion is furnished throughout in eastern style, matching its extravagant exterior.

Here you walk into a true wonderland. Nothing in Europe is quite like it.

Brighton was at first a simple fishing village but George III, who suffered from dyspepsia, was advised to try sea-bathing for his health and Brighton was one of the places he selected. As he left his bathing-hut each morning and walked gingerly into the sea, a small group of musicians followed him on a raft, playing 'God Save the King' in various keys and with many variations, so that royal dignity should be suitably maintained. In more recent times it was at Brighton, during the Second World War when its beaches were a maze of barbed wire and its

19

foreshore liberally mined, that General Montgomery set up his headquarters in preparation for liberating Europe. He chose a room in the Ship Hotel and lived a spartan life, sleeping on a camp-bed in the simplest of rooms in order to dispel any idea that the High Command deserved to live in luxury on account of its rank. When you are facing sudden death, the order of the day must be share and share alike.

In the far south-west of Sussex is Chichester, a Roman settlement where you can still see the original

Left: Brighton's Palace Pier is one of many such structures which once decorated British seaside resorts. Just as saints often lived on the top of columns in order to get closer to Heaven, so non-swimmers sought to get closer to the element which had helped to make Britain great. On piers the sea is all round and underneath you, and, on blustery days, some of it even splashes over the edge and lets you taste it.

Below left: The South Downs are one of the most satisfying stretches of open countryside in the whole of Britain, containing finely tilled farmland and woodland, quiet villages and relics of early man, including the Long Man of Wilmington (a sort of half-brother to Dorset's Cerne Abbas giant), hill forts and the bridges spanning the rivers that cut through this east-west ridge on their way to the sea. Rolling hills, villages, churches, farms, woods, cornfields, water meadows, flint mines – all are here, marked with centuries of steady occupation by man 'in a fair ground, a fair ground, yea Sussex by the sea'.

Below: Arundel Castle overlooks the river from which it takes its name. The Castle is the home of the Duke of Norfolk, Earl Marshal of England, who is responsible for the correct arrangements of all state occasions, especially the Coronation. When in 1901 Queen Victoria died after more than 63 years on the throne, the only person alive who had been present at her Coronation was a formidable German lady, the elder daughter of the Princess Augusta, Grand Duchess of Mecklenburg-Strelitz, who remembered the unusual procedures adopted at the Coronation of a monarch without a consort. Her memories were recorded and built into the pattern of the great celebration we know today.

street plan now overlaid and decorated with 1,500 years of elegant domestic architecture, including the Norman cathedral founded in 1075, which makes it one of the oldest in England. Close at hand are the remains of the Roman palace at Fishbourne, with fine mosaic pavements, only recently unearthed.

Inland the South Downs, with their glorious rural landscape, parks and villages, form an almost continuous

Above: Goodwood Racecourse is not the only attraction in this beautiful western part of the South Downs, the southern spur of chalkland marching eastwards to Beachy Head. Near Goodwood is the circuit where a noisier but no less exciting sport is pursued, Grand Prix motor-racing. But for historians the chief attraction must be Fishbourne, near Chichester. Here are the ruins of a palace occupied by Cogidubnus, a Roman viceroy of dubious loyalty who, in the conflict between Rome and the Saxon invaders, may have played off one side against the other. Certainly when they did conquer southern England, the Saxons seem to have had a fairly easy ride in the Fishbourne area.

Right: Chiddingstone is one of Britain's loveliest villages protected by the National Trust. This official body came into being in the early 1930s when people began to realize that many of the country's standing stones, cathedrals, castles, bridges and even factories – the positive evidence of the past and the people who created it – were gradually being destroyed and would, if not protected, disappear for ever in the remorseless march of so-called progress. So most of the beautiful places illustrated in this book now come under fierce public protection.

Below: A view of Canterbury Cathedral taken through one of the arches of the ruined Abbey which stands close by, shows the Bell Harry tower, so-called after the famous bell that hangs therein. The Cathedral is one of the glories of English architecture, begun in 1067 and added to over the following centuries. It was here that Archbishop Thomas à Becket was murdered by four of Henry II's henchmen in 1170. Thereafter it became a place of pilgrimage. Many of the pilgrims wore round their necks metal charms stamped out in the form of the Crucifixion. Some of these were dug up at Blackfriars close to the Mermaid Theatre in 1970. A few years ago, when I visited my old friend Bernard Pawley, Canterbury's Archdeacon, he let me sleep in Becket's bedroom inside the Cathedral precinct.

Right: Rye was a busy Channel port in the Middle Ages, but over the centuries the land has taken over from the sea as if in revenge for the sea eating away so many other coasts of eastern England. Rudyard Kipling wrote a lovely poem, 'A Smuggler's Song', warning residents not to be too inquisitive about the strange comings and goings at Rye's Mermaid Inn:
'If you wake at midnight, and hear a horse's feet,
Don't go drawing back the blind, or looking in the street,
Them that asks no questions isn't told a lie.
Watch the wall, my darling, while the Gentlemen go by!'
the 'Gentlemen' being gentlemen of the road, a polite name for smugglers or highwaymen. These old houses had plenty of hiding places for smuggled goods in their cellars, attics and back-yards.

24

Below: The cherry tree in full bloom confirms that this is Kent, the Garden of England. The characteristic oast houses are designed for drying, but not over-drying, hops, the flowers that give their peculiar flavour to British beer (the word oast *comes from an ancient Indian word meaning 'to heat' or 'to burn'). The hops are laid on trays and the flow of air is carefully regulated so that they are kept at precisely the right temperature. Hop-picking was once done by thousands of Londoners from the East End, who camped in and around the hop-fields, living in horse-drawn caravans or under canvas – mother, father and children all enjoying the fresh air and the opportunity to contribute to the family exchequer. Now the job is done by machines.*

Right above: Guildford on the River Wey, which cuts through the chalk hills extending from Wiltshire to Dover on its way to join the River Thames, boasts the ruins of a castle built by King Henry II, a fine cathedral, one of Britain's new universities and a range of fine period houses. But it stands high in my personal affections for its Civic Theatre, named the Yvonne Arnaud Memorial Theatre after the great Anglo-French comedienne, and modelled as to structure and mode of operation very much on the lines of London's Mermaid Theatre, which my wife and I built at Puddle Dock in 1959, adding to the theatre a high-class restaurant and thus offering patrons what we called 'an-all-in-evening-out'.

Right below: Village cricket, here being played in Surrey, is a mystery item for overseas visitors. There is great rivalry between neighbouring teams and matches are keenly contested. Before the First World War a group of literary celebrities captained by Herbert Farjeon formed a team, called I believe 'the Irregulars', whose aim was to visit as many as possible of England's loveliest villages. The season extended from mid-May to mid-September, so they saw England at its most superb. The tractor had not then replaced the horse, the pitch was often bumpy and the outfield unmown, but God was in His Heaven and all was right with the world. In July 1914 they disbanded, never to meet again.

band throughout West and East Sussex. The beautiful estates of Cowdray and Petworth, the Elizabethan Parham House, the Iron Age earthworks at Chanctonbury Ring, the medieval town of Steyning, Devil's Dyke, Graffham Down and Woolbeding, which has been called the 'greenest village in England', are some of the many attractions. Truly Sussex and Kent have been called the 'garden of England'. And just as Sussex had its iron mines in Roman times, so today Kent has its coal mines which are still being worked. Even in this luscious south-eastern corner of England, the facts of life bear hard upon the beauty spots.

Among the many enchanting buildings which grace the Weald, between the North and South Downs, is Penshurst Place in south-western Kent, one of the oldest and loveliest of all our stately homes. Parts of it date from the mid-14th century, and the owners have, over the years, tried to keep the great hall and other parts of the house much as they must have looked in Tudor times. This was the birthplace of Sir Philip Sidney (1554–86), the famous courtier poet of Queen Elizabeth's reign, who died fighting the Spaniards at the battle of Zutphen offering his water flask to a wounded private soldier with the immortal words: 'Thy need is greater than mine.' His descendant Lord de Lisle, the present owner of Penshurst, was one of the heroes of a later war, winning the Victoria Cross at Anzio, in Italy, in 1944.

West of Penshurst lie the Surrey Hills, another wonderland of chalk downs, spectacular views, tranquil villages and, nearby, sites on the old Pilgrim's Way, including the charming towns of Guildford and Farnham. North of Penshurst, around Chatham, is an area rich in associations with Charles Dickens. Nearby Chalk is the site described by Dickens in *Great Expectations* for the forge of blacksmith Joe Gargery, a part I played in David Lean's magnificent film adaptation in 1946.

Northern Surrey and north-western Kent contain dormitory suburbs of London, that 'flower of cities alle'. London grew up on the banks of the Thames and many of its most famous attractions are on or near the river. One of the most stirring sights at Greenwich, on the south

Above: The Tower of London was built by William the Conqueror to keep the capital and its citizens in subjection, and also to protect them from attack by pirates. It later became a royal prison. Traitors were rowed downstream and entered through Traitor's Gate. They were later beheaded on Tower Green. A long list of noble men and women suffered here, including Ann Boleyn, Lady Jane Grey, the Earl of Strafford, Sir Thomas More and Sir Walter Raleigh. Deep inside the Tower, beautifully displayed, heavily guarded and not to be missed are the Crown Jewels, comprising crowns, decorations and robes worn by the Royal Family on state occasions. The Queen's crown is surmounted by a large ruby worn by her predecessor Henry V at the Battle of Agincourt.

Left: The picture shows the prow of the three-masted sailing ship, Cutty Sark, at Greenwich, one of the famous 'clippers', which were made light, slim and fast in order to compete with the steamships threatening to put sailing ships out of business. They often raced each other home from China and the best of them, including Flying Cloud, Thermopylae, Lothair, Sir Lancelot, Wylo and Cutty Sark, often arrived neck and neck up the Channel, crowding on all sail. Cutty Sark is Scots for 'short shirt' and the ship's figurehead is a buxom girl in a daringly brief sort of chemise. I met Captain Woodger, Cutty Sark's last skipper, when his lovely ship was put into dry dock at Greenwich. He was then over 80. We went into his old cabin and the first thing he did was to feel behind the transom where he had left his pipe and tobacco tin 40 years previously. They were still there.

29

St Paul's Cathedral is the Christian power-house of the City of London, known affectionately as the 'Square Mile'. It replaced the medieval cathedral destroyed by the Great Fire in 1666 and most regard it as Christopher Wren's masterpiece. St Paul's Crypt houses the funeral carriage of the Duke of Wellington, the Tomb of Nelson, fragments of effigies that escaped the Fire, and memorial tablets to many renowned men and women, including Wren himself, whose plaque is inscribed Si monumentum requires, circumspice, *which loosely translated means 'If you're looking for my monument, take a look around the City and see the churches I built'. My wife and I lived in the Vestry house of one of them, St Magnus the Martyr on London Bridge.*

bank of the Thames, is the clipper ship *Cutty Sark*, launched in 1869, one of the best known of the square-riggers which carried wool from Australia and tea from China in the historic days of sail. Close at hand is Sir Francis Chichester's tiny *Gypsy Moth* in which the great modern mariner sailed single-handed around the world in 1966–67. The National Maritime Museum at Greenwich, besides being a majestic building in its own right, includes the first Royal Observatory, where standard time, called Greenwich Mean Time or GMT for short, was established.

From Greenwich regular boat services operate to Westminster via the magnificent Tower Bridge. Opened in the 1890s, this queen of bridges heralds the Tower of London, begun by William the Conqueror and often called 'the unhappiest building in Europe'. For 600 to 700 years, the Tower was used as a state prison. Prisoners were taken in through a low archway called Traitor's Gate

and were beheaded on a special mound called Tower Green. Many famous people perished there, including Anne Boleyn and Lady Jane Grey. Most prisoners submitted to the axe with great patience, but the Countess of Salisbury was so reluctant to die that she ran round and round the scaffold with the executioner chasing her, taking many swipes at her with his axe before he managed to finish her off.

Upstream, beyond the Tower, we suddenly catch sight of the vast dome of St Paul's Cathedral, which stands, like many of the City's famous buildings, including the Tower, Guildhall, the Bank of England, Mansion House, the Royal Exchange and the magnificent new Museum of London, to the north of the river. Theatre lovers will see on their left the sites of three famous Elizabethan playhouses, the Globe, the Hope and the Swan, all on the south side of the Thames. Then, on the north bank, is the famous Mermaid Theatre which

Covent Garden was formerly a fashionable piazza with one of London's only two theatres attached to it. It later became a marketplace for the sale of fruit and vegetables, and the original theatre was replaced by one of the world's great opera houses. In the early 1960s, when it was decided to close the market, local citizens fought a long battle to preserve the old, glass-roofed marketplace and its surrounding streets, full of pleasant shops and eating-houses. Their victory means that Covent Garden now retains much of its old flavour. The picture shows part of the original Floral Hall, once ablaze with flowers, but now full of happy Londoners enjoying a day out.

31

my wife and I and a few devoted friends built within a few steps of the site of the old Blackfriars Theatre, of which William Shakespeare himself was a seventh shareholder and which, having been used exclusively by the Queen's Men and then by the King's Men, can really claim to be the first, genuine Theatre Royal.

Beyond Blackfriars Bridge, we catch sight of the huge clock tower above the Houses of Parliament which contains the well-known bell, Big Ben. Nearby is Westminster Abbey, begun 900 years ago by King Edward the Confessor. This glorious Gothic cathedral shares with its comparatively younger sister, St Paul's, all national celebrations; mournings, christenings, weddings and coronations. Fronting the Thames are the Houses of Parliament designed in matching Gothic style by Augustus Pugin after its predecessor was burned down in 1832. Members of Parliament arrange for their constituents to join guided tours of this unique building, including Westminster Hall, one of the miracles of medieval woodwork, which was built by Hugh Herland, Richard's II's master-carpenter. There you can stand on the spot where Charles I faced his accusers and inspect the brass plates set in the floor to mark the spots where many of our kings and queens, and that great commoner Winston Churchill, have lain in state after their deaths.

A walk from the Houses of Parliament up Whitehall takes one past Downing Street, home of the prime

Left: St Katharine's Yacht Basin is in the restored St Katharine's Docks, a magnet for anyone who likes boats, on the north bank of the Thames downriver from Tower Bridge. After the docks had finally outlived their usefulness, decisions had to be made about various buildings surrounding them. Should they be pulled down or put to a fresh use? The 150-year-old warehouses, although originally utilitarian, are of such monumental dignity that they cried out for preservation. The restoration of the area was superbly carried out in the 1970s, and the basin around the buildings is now a nautical museum.

Above: Trooping the Colour is one of London's great sights, watched by the Prime Minister, members of the Government, retired servicemen and thousands of the general public. The Colour represents the regiment, just as in medieval times the coat of arms on shield and helmet stood for your leader. Every year, on the Queen's birthday, at a parade second only as a mixture of tear-jerker and heart-warmer to the gathering at the Cenotaph on Remembrance Sunday, the five regiments of foot guards, identifiable by the colour of their plumes and the number of buttons on each soldier's tunic, carry the Colours and offer their loyalty to Her Majesty who rides horseback into the arena and takes up her position to receive them.

Above: St James's Park is one of the most beautiful of London's open spaces, to be enjoyed by its citizens for rest, recreation and even innocent love-making. This gentleman, taking his ease on a warm autumn evening just before the gates are shut for the night, is typical of thousands who seek refuge from the noise and bustle of a great city – and nod off for half an hour. In warm weather thousands flock parkwards, shedding as many garments as they dare, and enjoying lunch-time sandwiches before flocking back to their offices.

Left: The Palace of Westminster, as the Houses of Parliament are officially known, is one of London's unique sights. The old Parliament was burned down in 1834 and two architects, Sir Charles Barry and Augustus Pugin, collaborated in creating a new one. Barry planned the overall arrangement, while Pugin undertook the decoration, producing thousands of drawings to confirm his conviction that the new building should match the glorious medievalism of the nearby Abbey, and the finished building turned out to be a masterpiece, as enchanting outside, especially now that it has been cleaned, as it is inside. Incorporated in the Palace is Westminster Hall (1399) where Charles I faced his accusers and where many recent monarchs have lain in state after death. The clock in Tom Tower is one of Europe's biggest, its chimes known and recognized the world over.

minister, with Sir John Vanbrugh's beautiful Admiralty building on the left, and Whitehall Palace on the right. It was here that Charles I was beheaded, and the window from which he stepped onto the scaffold on that bitterly cold morning in 1649 is still there. A little farther on is Hubert Le Sueur's magnificent equestrian statue of the martyred king and Trafalgar Square, dominated by Nelson's Column. On the far side of the square stands the National Gallery, which houses one of the world's great collections of European painting. I have only had space here to mention a few of London's many attractions. With its superb churches, palaces and other fine buildings, its many echoes of history, its lovely parks, and its rich cultural life, it is not surprising that London is Britain's principal tourist centre.

*Above: The Post Office Tower seen here in the background was built, even
though subconsciously, to confirm Britain's masculinity, as Dorset's
Cerne Abbas giant was intended to do for Stone Age man. Few people
would call it beautiful, but it is certainly different. No one can avoid
noticing it and wondering, as with the Albert Memorial, whose was the
brain that conceived it and why. It has a viewing platform and a revolving
restaurant on its top, but a bomb put these out of action a few years ago,
and the tower was closed to visitors for fear of further hazards.*

*Above left: Berwick Street Market, in Soho, harks back to the days when
London was smaller and more intimate, before broad, paved streets, cars,
shops and offices overwhelmed its village quality. As with the parks, the
authorities have managed to accommodate a good deal of unofficial activity
in such corners as Seven Dials, Islington, Pimlico, Petticoat Lane, and
here, almost in the heart of the capital. If you get to these places early and
go regularly to the same stall, you can save many pounds on your weekly
food bill.*

37

One of Buckinghamshire's beauty spots, Burnham Beeches, takes its name from its forest of that superb hardwood. This is chalk country and where there is chalk there are usually beech trees whose timber has always been much prized by the furniture trade, especially for the legs and rails of chairs and tables. Within easy reach of London, Burnham has for many years been a favourite haunt of day trippers, who go there to picnic and walk along the forest glades. In the early 1900s they travelled in horse-drawn wagons called 'brakes'. These simple vehicles yielded to the motor car, but day trips are still popular.

The Home Counties

I was born at Hayes End in what is now Greater London, and from here I acquired an early knowledge of the Home Counties. I knew that if I followed the main road westwards, I would come to Hillingdon's splendid St Margaret's Church with its tower of flint, and the Red Lion Inn where Charles I spent a night before retreating to the west with the Royalist Army. Then came Uxbridge with its Treaty House where the king parleyed with Oliver Cromwell, where the Metropolitan Railway had its terminus, and where Mr Gillies, the cutler, had in his shop window a knife with 365 blades made for the 1895 Paris Exhibition. Beyond Uxbridge lay Denham in Buckinghamshire, followed by Gerrard's Cross, Jordans and nearby Chalfont St Giles, where the poet John Milton lived for a while, and then lovely Beaconsfield.

Near Beaconsfield lay High Wycombe, home of men called *bodgers*, who made chairs from local beech trees. High Wycombe is cradled by the rolling chalklands that make up the Chiltern Hills and, wherever there is chalk, there are beech trees. The two go together 'like a knife and fork', as my father used to say. He was born in that area and, when he married my mother, he bought a set of eight chairs bodger-made out in the woods, with legs and rails of beech turned on a pole lathe, seats of elm shaped for the posterior with an adze, and backs of ash steamed and bent into a fine curve. There were two armchairs for my parents – father's was bigger than mother's – and six smaller ones for the family. My children still have some of them in their homes and they still do yeomen service. The set of eight chairs cost, if I remember rightly, only two guineas (£2.10).

To the south-west of my childhood home lay royal Windsor, in eastern Berkshire. Windsor is renowned not only for its castle, but also for its splendid Theatre Royal, where I worked as designer, scene-painter and small-part

This unusual view of Windsor Castle shows the carriageway leading to it through the Great Park. I served part of my theatrical apprenticeship at the Theatre Royal across the High Street in Windsor – as scene painter and small-part actor. There I met that great soldier Lord Alexander of Tunis, the theatre's patron. He confessed that, following a visit to the London Pavilion in the spring of 1914, he had conceived a passion to embrace the theatre as his way of life. But when the trouble with Germany blew up, he had to renounce that ambition. 'Lucky for us,' I said. 'Oh, I don't know,' he replied. 'No one is indispensable.'

actor in the mid-1930s under the banner and leadership of John Counsell, an old friend of my university days. The original, rather tumbledown Theatre Royal burned down in 1905, and Edward VII promised Queen Alexandra that he would replace it with the finest theatre in England. And so he did, even introducing the new-fangled electric light instead of gas lamps. But the electric current was of the direct rather than the alternating variety, and this nearly cost us the life of our chief electrician Cyril Douglas, who caught hold of two live wires and completed a circuit, burning off half of his two thumbs before we could switch off the current and release him. He spent five months in hospital, but then returned to the theatre for a further 40 years.

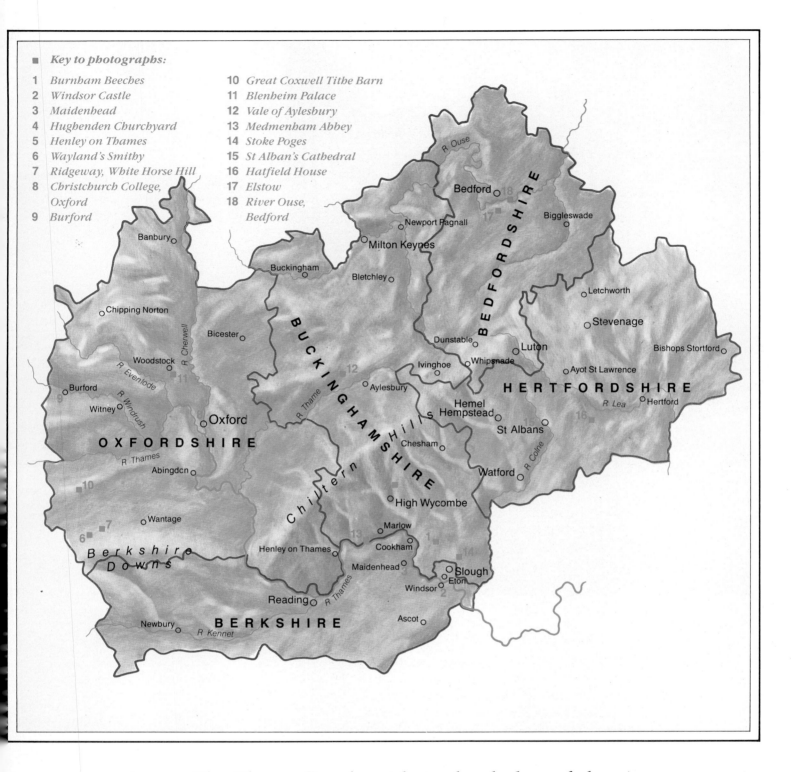

The Theatre Royal stands in the shadow of the superb Windsor Castle, which is not only beautiful in itself, but which also houses many artistic treasures. The Queen's Librarian, knowing my interest in pictures, sometimes got out a small selection of drawings by Leonardo, Raphael and Rembrandt and talked to me about them. Sometimes, great parties were held to celebrate important events, such as Britain's longstanding friendship with the Netherlands when, in the presence of the Dutch monarch, the glorious paintings by Van Dyck, including many of Charles I and Queen Henrietta Maria, were put on show.

Upriver from Windsor is Cookham, once the home of the painter Stanley Spencer. His disturbing paintings,

41

Above: Narrow boats wait their turn at Maidenhead to proceed through one of the locks on the River Thames for the annual expedition of swan-upping. All the swans on the river belong either to the Queen or to the Livery Companies of Vintners and Dyers, and have to be marked for identification, with nicks made in their beaks with a special tool – two nicks for the Dyers, three for the Vintners and none for the Queen. Every year boat-loads of officials from the Livery Companies go roving the river catching the new and unmarked swans, seizing them and making the required marks in their upper mandibles. They then hold a Swan Feast, a very ancient ceremony at which a number of elderly and uneatable birds are served.

Right: Hughenden near High Wycombe in Buckinghamshire was the home of the great Victorian statesman Benjamin Disraeli from 1847 until his death in 1881, when he was buried in the village churchyard. Disraeli is as great a name in the annals of the Tory Party as Gladstone is in the history of Liberalism. A Jewish politician who aspired to and achieved the office of prime minister was in those days a phenomenon, the more so as he also won the sympathy and approval of Queen Victoria by the art and grace of his bearing as well as by his brilliance. On the other hand, his arch-rival Gladstone, inflexibly Christian and dangerously liberal, never found Her Majesty's favour. Disraeli's greatest achievement was the purchase for Britain of a controlling interest in the Suez Canal, while Gladstone's was his far-seeing but unsuccessful championship of Irish Home Rule.

Below: The Tithe Barn at Great Coxwell in Oxfordshire is one of the masterpieces of medieval carpentry. Beautifully proportioned from the outside, its interior is a wonderland of oak beams, uprights and cross-pieces laced together in perfect harmony, supporting its stone roof with only a few light external buttresses. It was built in the 14th century by the monks of Beaulieu Abbey as a storehouse for grain, following the edict laid down in the Old Testament, proclaiming that a tithe (or tenth part) of everyone's earnings was owed to the church; this applied to harvests and hard cash.

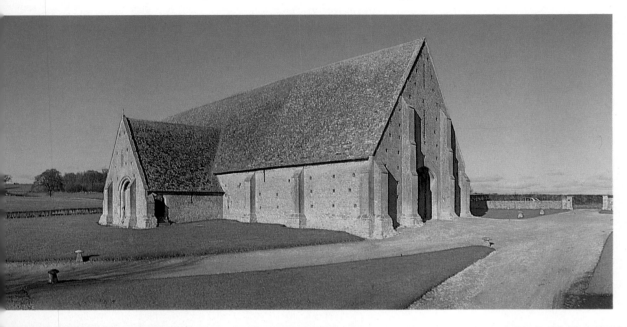

Wayland's Smithy is a prehistoric burial mound called a long barrow. This is a stone chamber, a sort of communal tomb filled with bodies, then roofed over and covered with earth. The bodies lie on shelves along with some of their personal belongings ready for use in the next world. Most peoples have believed in an after-life and have ensured that their dead find a few familiar objects when they awaken, some food and perhaps a ring, comb or knife. The trees were planted recently to give the site a human and friendly touch. After all these folk were our ancestors.

especially one showing in full swing the resurrection in a churchyard of people in 20th-century suits, bowler hats, nightgowns and straw boaters, was a healthy shock after the Old Masters of Windsor Castle. The Thames then snakes its way into Oxfordshire, passing through the Goring Gap which separates the chalk of the North Wessex Downs from the Chilterns. In south-western Oxfordshire, north of the lush Vale of White Horse, is the hamlet of Great Coxwell and the famous tythe barn, another glory of medieval carpentry. This great structure, used to store grain, once belonged to Beaulieu Abbey.

On to Oxford, where I spent three blissful years at Pembroke College, a humble seat of learning planted in the shadow of the mighty Christ Church. I made little impact on the academic scene at Oxford, but I fell under the spell of a great teacher, historian, philosopher and archaeologist, Robin Collingwood, whose influence has pervaded the rest of my life. I also made a number of faithful friends, whose love and wisdom have supported me ever since those early days.

Right: Henley-on-Thames in Oxfordshire is famed for its fine 18th-century five-arched bridge and for its yearly regatta, a river festival in which boats of various kinds row against each other, either one man per boat (single sculls), two per boat (pairs), four per boat (foursomes) or the mighty eights. Racing lasts for a whole week, which is known as Henley Week. The boats are called shells because of their lightness. If a boat-load of our Viking ancestors came back from the dead, I am sure they would doff their battle-gear and hurl down a challenge or two on the Henley towpath.

Right: Riders enjoy a morning out on the Ridgeway, White Horse Hill, south of Uffington in Oxfordshire. The Hill, which is named after the 374-foot (114-metre) long horse cut in the chalk in prehistoric times, is capped by an Iron Age castle. The horse and the bee were for many centuries sacred creatures – the horse because it could carry people tirelessly over long distances and had a remarkable memory for people and places, and the bee because its honey was the source of the delicious alcoholic drink called mead. Even more important, the bee could carry your soul up to Heaven on its strong wings. The broad, simple strokes with which the horse is drawn resemble the prehistoric figures painted in the French and Spanish caves of Lascaux and Altamira.

Below: Many of Oxford's colleges were founded in the days when Christianity ran like a steel cord through the whole of British life. Christ Church is the biggest of Oxford's colleges. It was built by Cardinal Wolsey when his master Henry VIII was engineering one of the greatest events in British history – the break with Rome and the establishment of the Church of England. This break, regrettable in so many ways, forced the British to become great ship-builders and great sailors in order to protect themselves against a fiercely hostile Continent. Nestling at the feet of Christ Church is my own college Pembroke, humble in size and resources but mighty in character.

Below: The Vale of Aylesbury, lush lowland country rich in pasture and hedgerow with well-watered clay soils, is perfectly suited for farming and stock-rearing. It boasts the biggest single field in Britain, the 300-acre (121-hectare) Creslow Great Field. When the London, Midland and Scottish Railway first came to the Vale of Aylesbury, Lord Rothschild, who lived in the vast mansion of Mentmore, is said to have insisted that the railway should not come any nearer to his home than Cheddington, 3 miles (5 km) away; and that the Rothschild family should have free first-class tickets to and from London for life as part rental for the wayleave. This shows how hard it was for the carriage trade to adjust to the Puffing Billy. On Queen Victoria's first train ride, her coachman rode on top of the engine, clasping the funnel with his bare hands. He descended at the end of the trip plastered with smut and with a pair of very sore mitts.

49

From Ivinghoe, I explored the neighbouring counties of Bedfordshire and Hertfordshire. I once bicycled to an auction at Leighton Buzzard in Bedfordshire and returned with a Windsor chair, a horse brush and a Stilton cheese for five shillings (£0.25). Sometimes we would climb to the top of Beacon hill, where I would tell my daughter Sally why the ancient Britons built fortresses on defensible hilltops. Or we would travel to the delightful Whipsnade Zoo in southern Bedfordshire, whose open countryside populated by animals is so much to be preferred, in my opinion, to the formal zoo in London's Regent's Park.

Framed by a particularly fine lych-gate is the church of Stoke Poges in Buckinghamshire. The word lych comes from an old German word meaning body. The roofed lych-gate was big enough to shelter a coffin and a few mourners until the priest arrived to lead the sorrowing procession up the pathway into the church and then to the graveside for the actual internment. Here at Stoke Poges the poet Thomas Gray wrote one of the most famous of English poems, his celebrated 'Elegy in a Country Churchyard'.

St Alban's Cathedral is dedicated to a Roman soldier Alban, reputed to have been martyred for embracing Christianity; and much of the stone for building the Cathedral probably came from the ruined Roman theatre nearby. The official religion of the Romans, who ruled Britain for more than 300 years, was Mithraism, the worship of the Sun and the sealing of that worship in the blood of a slaughtered bull. It must have taken a very brave man to renounce that worship.

South-east of Ivinghoe lay St Albans in Hertfordshire, named after Britain's earliest saint, and boasting the remains of a Roman theatre and an abbey with the longest nave in Europe. The citizens of St Albans played a big part in the Peasants' Revolt of 1381, when the working people of the southern counties rose against their greedy rulers, captured London and beheaded London's Bishop Simon Sudbury, whose head is preserved in Sudbury Parish Church in Suffolk, and nearly toppled the kingdom. The chief leaders were Wat Tyler and John Ball, but the people of St Albans had a local leader, Richard Grindcobbe, who also died on the gallows.

North of St Albans is Knebworth House, home of the Victorian novelist Lord Lytton. Many generations of Lyttons are buried in a church which stands inside the park, as if to keep each other company and remain in constant communication regardless of the grave, a heartening thought.

East of St Albans is Hatfield House, another of England's truly stately homes. It was built between 1608 and 1612 by Robert Cecil, 1st Earl of Salisbury. Its present owner, the Marquess of Salisbury, is one of that illustrious company who, when taxation threatened them with ruin, turned part of their homes into a private dwelling and opened the rest for the enjoyment of the

The old Tudor palace of Hatfield, from this point of view, looks more like a tithe-barn than an ancestral home. But it is a building of great beauty, built for the Bishops of Ely and taken over by Henry VIII when he dissolved the monasteries. Thereafter, it became the principal country residence of the Tudors. Queen Elizabeth I lived here as a child and it was here that she heard of the death of her sister Mary Tudor and of her own accession to the throne. When making one of her frequent progresses around the great homes of her subjects, she often included Hatfield in her itinerary. It was and still is the home of the famous Salisbury family.

public. Today visitors can imagine themselves lords and ladies living in a glorious past, sleeping in four-poster beds, treading on thick carpets, dining by the light of glittering chandeliers with footmen in attendance, or strolling over the beautiful lawn. Kings and queens once paid regular visits to their subjects' great houses, and the noblemen who owned them spared no expense to give their monarchs a memorable time.

Another lovely spot near St Albans is Ayot St Lawrence, which contains Shaw's Corner, home of one of Britain's leading dramatists, Bernard Shaw, from 1906 until his death in 1950. I never met Shaw myself, but a year or two after his death, I came to know Blanche Patch, who had been his devoted secretary for more than thirty years. I asked her if she could find me one of his autographs for my collection and she told me that I could have as many as I liked, because she had cut off and preserved all the signatures from his used cheques. 'I sell them for ten shillings each,' she said. 'You see, he was very rich, but like so many rich people, very mean and I suspected that he wouldn't leave me much in his will. I now sell these signatures to keep myself going.' I bought a couple of dozen. Miss Patch spent her last days in a humble hotel in Kensington, London, where she wrote a book called *My Thirty Years with GBS*. She told me how she discovered that Shaw was colour-blind. 'You see,' she said, 'he had a green jacket which got worn through at the elbows and he asked me to mend it. I couldn't find any green stuff, so I stitched in pieces of dark blue material and he never noticed the difference.'

Elstow, Bedfordshire, was the home of John Bunyan, author of The Pilgrim's Progress *and one of the greatest of English writers. A tinker by trade, he became a renowned local preacher and spent 11 years in Bedford jail for spreading his radical beliefs. The Pilgrim's Progress, an allegory of man's journey through all the hazards of life to the Promised Land, was a small, inexpensive volume written for simple working folk. But it was so popular that only a single copy of its first edition survives. As I was brought up a Baptist, it was one of the first books I ever heard of, and I believe that with a day or two's practice I could still recite most of it by heart. An iron fiddle and other relics of this great Englishman can be seen in a local museum.*

The River Great Ouse runs through Bedford, crossing verdant pastureland
before entering the Wash near King's Lynn. Bedford's Member of
Parliament in the early 1800s, the renowned Samuel Whitbread, was the
inventor of an advanced poor law system, proposing government aid for the
unemployed. He also borrowed cash to rebuild London's Drury Lane
Theatre, but when the theatre failed he shot himself. Just east of Bedford is
Cardington, where the rigid airship R-101 was built, only to crash on its
maiden flight in 1930. Cardington has a bridge commissioned by Samuel
Whitbread from an engineer from Yorkshire, John Smeaton. Smeaton was
the designer of the third Eddystone Lighthouse, all previous attempts
having met with disaster. But Smeaton hit on the idea of treating the stone
blocks in mortise and tenon fashion, interlocking them both vertically and
horizontally, so that the harder the sea punched them, the tighter they
locked together.

55

St Osyth's Priory, near Clacton in Essex, has the lightness of pure Gothic structures, reaching for Heaven instead of embracing the earth-like Romanesque. You can imagine it lifting off and floating away. It was founded in memory of an East Anglian king beheaded by the Danes in AD 653 for being a Christian. His wife Osyth founded the abbey in his memory and later she herself became a saint. Behind this delicate facade are public gardens where you can wander and imagine yourself listening to the pad of human feet down the night stairs and voices from long ago chanting the Holy Office.

The Eastern Counties

If I were asked to give a snap definition of Britain, I would say that it is a collection of islands lying to the west of Europe and that it's full of churches. And if I were required to name my favourite, I would choose the tiny Saxon church of St Peter's-on-the-Wall at Bradwell on Sea, in eastern Essex. To my way of thinking, there seems to be more solid belief, more devotion and more Christianity per cubic inch packed into Bradwell than anywhere else in Britain.

Away to the north, the city of Norwich, Norfolk's county town, boasts not only a magnificent cathedral, but also about 40 parish churches of supreme beauty built between 1200 and 1500, many of them containing some of the most glorious stained glass ever made. If I were not already a Christian, a morning at Bradwell followed by a week in Norwich would turn me into one.

For hundreds of years, the wealth of the eastern counties, comprising East Anglia, a former kingdom consisting roughly of modern Norfolk and Suffolk, Cambridgeshire and Essex, was based on wool. The woolmasters grew rich and built fine churches as acts of piety and thanksgiving. But in the 18th and 19th centuries, the region turned to arable farming. Its fertile lands became the breadbasket of the Industrial Revolution.

By their joint efforts, four men contrived to effect a corresponding revolution in British agriculture. First there was Thomas Coke of Holkham (East Anglia's noblest house), who held an annual agricultural festival to which farmers and landowners from all over Europe were invited. Then Robert Bakewell of Leicestershire, who increased by twice or thrice the size of local sheep and thus their yield of meat and fleece. Third Viscount Townshend, who pioneered the growing and storage of turnips for winter feed, and who was known to a fellow

*St Peter's Chapel, Bradwell on Sea, Essex, is a tiny, barn-like structure
built by St Cedd who was sent down from the north by St Cuthbert to
convert the East Saxons in AD 654. He used stones from the ruins of the
nearby Roman fort at Othona. This church is so simple, so functional, so
devoid of decoration that I can imagine Joseph and Mary pausing there for
the night. And I can imagine Jesus being born there among bales of straw,
with the cattle dropping to their knees in salutation and weeping with joy
at His birth, and with sorrow at the foreknowledge of His death, while
farm-hands pay their respects and bring Him a ball, a rattle and a lamb's
wool blanket for Mary to tuck Him up for the night. The trappings of
Christianity are all very well, but the Bible tells us that Jesus was born in a
cattle-shed and laid in a manger. To my mind that is one of the greatest
things about it.*

farmer, King George III, as 'Turnip Townshend'. Finally there was Jethro Tull, who was born in Berkshire and who invented the seed drill, making it possible to sow (and weed) the fields in rows instead of at random.

Essex is a low-lying county. Much of it was once forested, but little forest remains, except in the south-west of the county. This is Epping Forest, the hunting ground of Saxon, Norman and Tudor monarchs who shot deer with bow and arrow from structures like skeleton houses on stilts, in perfect safety, with food and drink supplied. Eastern Essex is flat, with many creeks,

59

mud flats and drowned estuaries full of duck, geese and wading birds, which are more or less safe from man only because he happens not to be a wader.

Among the cities of Essex, Colchester in the north-east was famed as one of the finest Roman settlements north of the Alps. It was assaulted and captured in AD 60 by Queen Boudicca (or Boadicea as we once called her),

Epping Forest in Essex is part of an ancient royal hunting ground. The Norman kings were great huntsmen and large areas of Essex were reserved for their pastime. Their special quarry was red deer and they alone could hunt them. Poachers were often savagely punished, losing a hand or even their eyes. The trees were protected by men called verderers, who also had to watch out for poachers and lead the hunt to places where deer were to be found. The royal hunting lodges in the forests were oak-framed, roofed cottages with the top storey wide open so that court ladies could watch the hunt and, if possible, see and applaud the actual kill.

Left: Maldon in Essex is an attractive and busy seaside town devoted largely to fishing. It is famous in history for a bloody battle fought here in AD 991 between the British and an army of Vikings who had camped on the island lying just offshore. After three days of fierce encounter the Vikings were victorious and the British retired to lick their wounds.

Below: The Saxons, unlike the Romans, were seafarers, not settlers. They built mainly with the material they understood – timber. But timber rots and burns, so most of their domestic buildings have disappeared. The nave of this tiny Essex church at Greensted-by-Ongar is the only surviving example. It is made of oak beams split down the middle and then placed edge to edge to form a continuous wall. The eaves kept it dry and successive builders found it firm enough to continue its sacred function, for the word nave is derived from a Greek word meaning ship or ark.

whose followers had come to hate Roman occupation. She waited until the Roman commander, Suetonius Paulinus, was away, leading his troops against the rebellious Welsh. But on hearing of the revolt Paulinus made a forced march across Britain, arrived unexpectedly, and cut the British army to pieces. Boudicca fled to nearby woods, killed her two daughters, and then committed suicide. Colchester's ancient heritage is still evident in its many Roman remains and splendid museum.

In north-western Essex is Thaxted, a famous village with a superb 14th-century church as big as a cathedral. Here, in the 1920s, a great clergyman, Conrad Noel, preached Christian Communism, and even flew a red flag from his church spire. But Cambridge University students invaded Thaxted, climbed the spire, and substituted a Union Jack. Battle raged in the streets and many heads were broken. Another revolutionary, John Ball, one of the leaders of the 14th-century Peasants'

Revolt, is said to have lived in a tiny chapel above the main door of the church. Perhaps it was here that he wrote his immortal couplet:

> 'When Adam delved and Eve span
> Who was then the gentleman?'

Thaxted also has a superb Moot Hall, with a public lockup, where drunks and disorderly citizens could be stowed for the night. It also boasts many splendid medieval houses of timber with plaster infill, much of it decorated with patterns in low relief called pargetting.

Scenic countryside enriches Dedham Vale on the Essex-Suffolk border. This section of the Stour valley is associated with two of England's greatest painters: John Constable, whose rural scenes had a considerable influence on French impressionism, born at East Bergholt; and Thomas Gainsborough, born in Sudbury, farther upstream. These are not the only artists of the eastern counties. In northern Norfolk lived the 19th-century Norwich School of Watercolourists, led by John Crome, John Sell Cotman, and Peter de Wint. Many of their finest paintings adorn local museums.

Left: The tiny, 350-year-old Sun Inn in Saffron Walden, Essex, has broad eaves and an upper storey overhanging 2 feet (0.6 metres) above the lower in order to gain extra space upstairs. Houses like these, often with a third overhanging storey so that people could almost shake hands across the street, were typical of Shakespeare's London.

How vivid is Borachio's line in Much Ado About Nothing: 'Stand thee close, then, under this pent-house, for it drizzles rain'. The Sun Inn is faced with plaster pargetting, a word derived from the French jetter, meaning to throw. This was because builders once threw plaster onto a wall any-old-how. But then they began to think how much nicer it would look if it was ornamented, as here with interlocking arches and ropes of flowers, like the icing on a Christmas cake.

Below: Flatford Mill, Dedham Vale, Suffolk, is familiar to most of us from John Constable's famous painting of it which, along with his pictures of 'The Hay Wain' and 'Willy Lott's Cottage', helped to change the whole vocabulary of European painting. What matters is the overall shock, tone and feel of a picture – in other words, the impression it makes when you first see it. To recognize the importance of this required a very special pair of eyes and a special skill and sensitivity in transferring to the canvas what those eyes were seeing, so that other people could see the world in a new light, as he was seeing it. Great painters like Constable can be described as people who offer to share their eyesight with humanity at large.

Left: Standing on the site of a former malt house in which barley was prepared for brewing, the Maltings at Snape, Suffolk, is a fine timber building (rebuilt after a fire in 1969), which was converted into a theatre-cum-concert hall by Benjamin Britten, greatest of all English composers. Here he and his friends organized yearly festivals of classical music, contemporary as well as early. The festivals soon gained world-wide acclaim and artists of international repute were proud to perform there. The poet George Crabbe was born at nearby Aldeburgh and it was upon his poem 'The Borough' (1810) that Britten based his masterpiece Peter Grimes.

*Above: The Post Mill at Saxtead Green in Suffolk is one of the few
remaining examples of a windmill still in working order out of perhaps
10,000 in the mid-19th century. Mill House, Mill Cottage, Mill Rise,
Mill Corner, Mill Lane, Mill Hill and Mill Wall bear witness to their
number and importance, not forgetting the hundreds of families named
Mills and Miller. My wife and I lived for years at the Mill House in
Little Barfield, Essex, a charming house, but the mill had burned
down 50 years previously and had never been replaced. If windmills and
watermills had not been as plentiful as villages in the Middle Ages, the
population would have gone hungry. I have a pair of miller's spectacles,
made of fine, meshed wire, for the mills were often so full of dust that
millers could hardly see.*

*Left: The Bridge of Sighs, Cambridge, is almost a replica of the well-
known Bridge of Sighs in Venice. It spans the River Cam, after which
Cambridge was named. In the water below the bridge, small parties of
undergraduates enjoy river outings in oared skiffs or in boats known as
punts. These are flat-bottomed craft propelled and steered from the stern of
the craft by a long pole thrust into the river bed and then withdrawn ready
for the next thrust. A trip on the river by punt was once one of the few
permitted ways of meeting female friends, except for tea or an occasional
college dance. But the last 40 years have witnessed a great loosening of
those bonds. The Oxford Eight once employed a highly successful and
knowledgeable female cox; we await the first female stroke with keen
anticipation.*

67

Along the Suffolk coast is Aldeburgh, former home of Benjamin Britten, one of Britain's greatest composers. His masterpiece, *Peter Grimes*, has its setting in the very seascape where its composer lived and died. Britten and his friend, the tenor Peter Pears, were founders of the annual Aldeburgh Festival, which is mounted in a converted 19th-century malthouse.

In north-western Suffolk is Bury St Edmunds, a city named after and dedicated to the memory of its patron saint, who was murdered by the Danes in the ninth century. It has a fine cathedral and many splendid private houses, but its glory is its vast stone gatehouse, all that remains of its medieval abbey. The sheer size of this structure gives an unforgettable impression of the power of the Roman Catholic Church in its prime, a power with which Henry VIII battled and overturned when he broke with Rome and dissolved the monasteries.

Bury St Edmunds is not far from the border with Cambridgeshire, whose university town has just as many

Above: Downing College, like most colleges in Cambridge, is a noble, classical structure surrounded by lawns, trees and flowerbeds, a perfect place in which to pursue a journey along the established paths of learning. Such journeys do not always run smooth. For thousands of people, Downing is now remembered for its great maverick teacher of English Literature, Frank Leavis, who brought a fresh clarity and rigour to the study of our language, from which Cambridge has not yet recovered, nor forgiven him. He was a born teacher and, when his message met with official disapproval, he set up his little podium in Cambridge's market square and lectured in the open air, to large and attentive crowds.

Above right: Ely Cathedral, towering out of the fenlands of Cambridgeshire, is one of the most satisfying of cathedrals, because it has not been greatly tidied up, or 'improved', like many other churches and historic buildings. Its chief glory is its timber lantern erected by the cathedral's surveyor Alan of Walsingham, following the collapse of the cathedral's spire in 1322. No one knows exactly how workmen managed to lift the eight massive oak beams into position, but a small model in the south transept suggests as a possible method a huge pulley wheel and a long rope pulled by horses from meadows outside the buildings. The picture shows the west front of the cathedral with the octagonal lantern in the background.

dreaming spires as its rival, Oxford. The colleges of Cambridge are rich in Biblical names, including King's (whose glorious chapel boasts a world-famous choir), Trinity, Jesus, St. John's and Christ's.

North of Cambridge is Ely, capital of the semi-marshland known as the Fens, where Hereward the Wake held out against the Normans until he was betrayed. The glory of Ely is its cathedral, and the glory of the cathedral is its octagonal lantern, consisting of eight huge oak beams lifted into the space formerly occupied by a stone tower, which one night in the 14th century collapsed and fell into the cathedral itself. The cathedral surveyor Alan of Walsingham conceived the idea of substituting a timber structure for the ruined spire – an engineering feat of unparalleled audacity and complexity. The oak beams came from the New Forest and, so far as can be ascertained, were lifted into position by a team of horses harnessed to a cable running over a huge wheel and pulled from well outside the cathedral. Ely has a special beauty

69

because, of all British cathedrals, it has never been 'improved' or 'tidied up', and it seems to have grown out of the earth on which it sits.

East of Cambridgeshire is the large and mostly flat county of Norfolk. In the north-west are the ancient port-cum-market town of King's Lynn and Sandringham, one of the Queen's private homes. She and the rest of the Royal family go to Sandringham for brief spells to rest and recuperate for the next excruciating round of public duty, which is carried out with such humour and unwavering devotion.

This part of Norfolk has one of England's longest and loveliest stretches of coastline and hinterland. Inland is the world-famous Shrine of Our Lady of Walsingham. Here the Mother of Jesus appeared in 1061 to Lady Richeld, the lady of the manor, and commanded her to establish the shrine. Since then Walsingham has been an important place of pilgrimage.

In eastern Norfolk are the famous Broads, a series of tranquil lakes and waterways, beloved of holiday-makers who enjoy boating and the rough and tumble of life afloat. These lakes and waterways were once thought to be natural features, but they are now known to be the remains of medieval peat diggings. In south-western Norfolk is a wilderness called Breckland. Here are

Wicken Fen, part of a formerly much larger water-logged area south of The Wash, is jealously guarded as a unique region of natural beauty. Persistent and long-standing attempts to drain the fenlands by windmill, mechanical pump and the cutting of canals to divert superfluous water have gradually reclaimed most of the area. But scattered villages on firm land, a few trees, more sky than anywhere in Europe and a profusion of wildlife give the Fens a unique character. The local hero, Hereward the Wake, held out against the Normans for four years after the Conquest. He had his headquarters somewhere among these impassable bogs and creeks, until a traitor led the enemy to his hideout and he was captured. It is said that William the Conqueror pardoned him as a reward for his skill and daring.

Sandringham, Norfolk, embodies a 7,000-acre (2,833-hectare) estate, a magnificent house and a number of local villages, and is used by the Royal Family as their holiday home. I once had a wonderful dream about it. I was working as a gardener at Buckingham Palace, and the Queen invited me to go to spend a weekend with them. 'We're having trouble with our hydrangeas' she said, 'and I'd like you to see what's wrong. I'm afraid you'll have to go in the boot', she said, 'because the rest of the car is full up', so of course I said I'd be delighted to lend a hand and I clambered in, just as I was, and off we went. But the driver missed the turning to King's Lynn and we went on to Skegness, and when Prince Philip opened the boot we were in Butlins! Prince Philip wanted to go back, but the Queen would not hear of it. She said 'she'd always wanted to try Butlins'. So we stayed and I was invited to be their guide and we had a wonderful time – 'Wakey, wakey, wakey, rise up and shine!' and the roller coaster and the dodgem cars, and Prince Charles insisted on being a Red-Coat and Her Majesty said 'how happy she'd been spending the day with her people'. And she congratulated me on being such an excellent guide and said I deserved to be made Lord!

Left: Norwich Cathedral is one of the finest in Britain, its nave and tower being perfect examples of massive Norman work, while its spire is 15th-century. The city itself boasts 30-odd attendant churches, many of them masterpieces of medieval stone and timberwork, adorned by superb stained glass. As with all cathedrals, one must wonder what kind of people built them, and how deep was their faith in God and in the timber scaffolding upon which the whole construction depended. Many a mason must have plunged to his death during the 500 years of Britain's cathedral-building. But as the poet Francis Quarles says, in describing how Zachaeus scrambled down from the tree to get closer to Jesus: 'Nor could he fall unless he fall to Heaven.'

Above right: Do not think that because the Norfolk Broads are inland waters they are not subject to wind and weather. The boat in the background is lying close inshore and is partly sheltered. But the one in the foreground has ventured into the open and has been caught in a light puff of wind – nothing violent but enough to make the boat heel over to port, a warning that even here you should not let your children go sailing without a life-jacket.

Right: Lowestoft is primarily a holiday resort, but many of its inhabitants are fishermen and its lifeboat station was built about a quarter of a century before the foundation of the Royal National Lifeboat Institution. It is claimed that in winter there is nothing between Lowestoft and the North Pole. But summer brings holiday-makers here and to Oulton Broad to the west. Oulton Broad is the southernmost of these popular inland waterways, much favoured by those seeking a spell on the water but not quite experienced or daring enough to try the open sea.

Grimes' Graves, a series of pits from which prehistoric miners extracted flint for arrow-heads, fish-hooks, bracelets and other ornaments, and for making sparks which start a fire. The pits were in use well into the present century.

The coasts of Norfolk, Suffolk and Essex contain many holiday resorts. Cromer and Sheringham in Norfolk and Frinton in Essex were traditionally centres for the better-off, while Clacton and Southend in Essex were for the 'lower orders' (a phrase unique to the English language). Many early photographs of these resorts show ladies and gentlemen in well-fitting swimsuits, sporting around bathing huts. These contrast with pictures of Londoners, who have taken off their shoes and stockings and tucked up their skirts and petticoats, paddling in the sea and building sandcastles with their children.

To show how highly prized are such resorts as Clacton, let me recall a story told by my sister, who was for many years a primary Sunday School teacher at Hayes Salem Chapel in Middlesex. One day she ventured to describe to her class of 40 or so six- to seven-year-olds what Heaven was like – the colour, the beating of angels' wings, the trumpets sounding, and millions of voices praising God. Never doubting for a moment a majority response, she said: 'Now, how many of you would like to come with me to Heaven?' And every little hand shot up like lightning except one, a lad named Willie Sibley, who kept his arms folded. 'Oh, Willie,' said my sister, deeply disappointed, 'you don't want to come to Heaven? Why ever not?' 'Please miss,' replied Willie, his lips quivering and the tears now beginning to fall, 'our mum's taking us to Clacton.'

Far left: Peaceful beaches and many places of great interest are within easy reach of Brancaster, in north-west Norfolk. To the east is Burnham Thorpe, birthplace of Lord Nelson, Holkham Hall where Lord Coke held his yearly Farming Festivals which helped to revolutionize British agriculture, and Walsingham where, in 1061, Lady Richeld had her vision of the Virgin Mary and which thereafter became a shrine and a place of pilgrimage. To the south is Sandringham, one of the private homes of the Royal Family, and Castle Rising with its fine Norman castle and a name better known as that of a famous hymn tune which I learned at my mother's knee: it begins 'The roseate hues of early dawn . . .'

Left: The tying and cutting of reeds for roof thatching in Norfolk is an example of how raw materials from close at hand have been traditionally used, rather than those from far away. This principle has underlain the whole of British national life. Other indicators are tiles, slate and thatch – whether it be reed, corn, heather or ling – for roofing. The thatcher here has finished the span on his left and is preparing the foundation for the next span. Thatch has to be thick like an overcoat and the foundation must be beaten down hard before the top layers are added. A thatched roof can be as much as 18 inches (46 cm) thick and great thatchers reveal their artistry by building the top layers into patterns and even adding decorative bunches, called finials, at both ends of the ridge.

Below: Hunstanton is an east coast town with the distinction of facing west and enjoying spectacular sunsets over the sea. It is also the only resort that accommodates Britain's two cultures for, along with its hotels and solid residential area, it boasts a funfair and a caravan park, so that the two life-styles merge into one another like water-colours on a sheet of damp paper. Holme next the Sea, a little farther north, has a fine bird observatory and, in the autumn, migrants on their way to warmer, southern climes make this their first stop-over.

Sea traffic between Holland and East Anglia naturally encouraged not only architectural, but also agricultural exchanges. East Anglia was flat, the soil was just right, the know-how was available and the stock was only a short sea voyage away. So Lincolnshire fell naturally into bulb growing and here at Surfleet, just north of Spalding, it is at its most intense. Lincolnshire also boasts its glorious wolds, some of the richest crop and sheep-farming country in Britain, lightly populated and varied in landscape, and falsely credited with being flat when in reality it is happily balanced between hill and valley.

The East Midlands

King John's treasure is supposed to lie buried somewhere in the semi-marshland adjoining the Wash between King's Lynn in Norfolk and Boston in Lincolnshire. In early times, kings and queens took all their belongings with them when they travelled, including wagonloads of furniture, royal robes, crowns and jewels, writing materials, cooking utensils and even chamber pots. King John's baggage train foundered in the mud. Wagons and their drivers and horses with their riders went under along with the treasure. There it still lies, and people with long rods and metal detectors are still trying to find it.

Boston itself is famous for its cathedral-like church, St Botolph's. Its single tower thrust up into the sky is called the Boston Stump, and its prominence in this flat landscape has made it a useful landmark for sailors. Much of Boston's domestic architecture, especially its brickwork, is Dutch in appearance because, like King's Lynn, Boston had strong trading links with Holland, and there has been much interchange between their ways of life and ours.

On the coast north-east of Boston, there are stretches of sand dunes, nature reserves and several attractive coastal resorts, including Skegness with its renowned Butlin's Holiday Camp. Sir Billy Butlin realized that such simple and invigorating places were necessary for people in need of rest and relaxation, pleasant company and good food and plenty of fun. He also understood that people enjoy being organized. So he established properly programmed camps run to time-tables, with a wide choice of facilities to suit everybody, including restful areas for the aged and infirm, television rooms, giant dining halls and intimate public houses. These vast complexes are controlled by loudspeakers and an army of courteous assistants, called redcoats, who are

Boston Stump, Lincolnshire, is the 272-foot (83-metre) high Gothic tower of
St Botolph's Church, more like a cathedral than a mere family church, and
a landmark for many miles around. The virtue of Gothic architecture is
that it was never riveted to any particular set of rules. Instead it was
inspired by religious passion, freedom of decoration and reckless invention,
all of which led to flying buttresses, unrivalled carpentry and the
astonishing range of design and ornament which are its hall-marks. Way
back in 1940 I spent a happy two weeks in Boston, shooting the canal
scenes in Michael Powell's film One of Our Aircraft Is Missing.
Michael chose Boston because its domestic architecture resembles that of
Holland where our aircraft was supposed to have ditched.

Peak District

Buxton 14

16

15

Chesterfield

Worksop

R Trent

Gainsborough

Mablethorpe

Lincoln Wolds

3 Lincoln

Horncastle

Skegness 4

Matlock

R Derwent

Mansfield

NOTTINGHAMSHIRE

LINCOLNSHIRE

R Dove

DERBYSHIRE

Sherwood Forest

Southwell

Newark-on-Trent

R Witham

Ilkeston

13

12

Nottingham

Boston

Derby

Long Eaton

Belvoir

Grantham

The Wash

R Trent

2

Loughborough

Melton Mowbray

Spalding

Coalville

9

LEICESTERSHIRE

11

Bosworth Field ✕

Leicester

Stamford

10

R Welland

Hinckley

8

7

Fotheringhay

5

Market Harborough

Corby

NORTHAMPTONSHIRE

Kettering

R Nene

Wellingborough

Daventry

Northampton

6

Key to photographs:

1 Boston Stump
2 Tulip field, Surfleet
3 Lincoln Cathedral
   East Window, Lincoln Cathedral
4 Skegness
5 Fotheringhay
6 Stoke Bruerne
   Stoke Park
7 Rockingham Castle
8 Grand Union Canal, Foxton
9 Bradgate Park
10 Uppingham Church
11 Rutland rural scenery
12 Nottingham
13 Wollaton Hall
14 Buxton
15 Chatsworth
16 Rushup Edge
17 Beresford Dale

eager to meet your every need, and are not unlike the ex-Royal Marines employed in the House of Lords to perform the same invaluable services. I have performed at Skegness and have marvelled at the floods of pure pleasure offered to hard-pressed working folk at extremely reasonable prices. Billy Butlin was one of the great figures of our time, a true benefactor of humanity.

Behind Lincolnshire's lovely coastlands are the glorious Lincolnshire Wolds, rolling chalklands dissected by deep, tranquil valleys swathed in beechwoods.

Above: Skegness, in 1875 a modest
fishing village with 134 inhabitants, is
now the most popular seaside resort in
Lincolnshire, catering for hundreds of
thousands each year. It gained and
maintains its popularity through its
fine, bracing air, the down-to-earthness
of its people and the biggest and best
of the renowned Billy Butlin's holiday
camps. Skegness has all you could
desire in the way of popular appeal –
a fine promenade, amusement arcades,
public gardens, golf courses, cock-shies
– the lot. If you want to see how the
solid core of the British population
enjoys its summer break, let your hair
down and try Skegness; if you want a
change, walk westwards onto the
Lincolnshire Wolds and enjoy Britain
at its deepest and richest, mile after
mile of space and sky, with low,
rolling farmland full of cattle and
sheep.

Above: Lincoln Cathedral is an example of Gothic architecture at its most spacious and coherent, with wide variation of design and decoration, dictated not by compass and straight edge but achieved through instinct and feeling.

Much of it was discussed and agreed between abbot, surveyor and stone-mason, possibly sketched out on a piece of vellum, then discussed further between master-mason and his mates, and finally 'to work!' with a confident assertion: 'We'll get the feel of it as we go along.' If the original Goths, wild and untutored horsemen from the steppes of Russia who brought Rome to its knees but whose only significant contribution to civilization was the invention of the stirrup, could see how their name had come to be used, they would turn in their graves and claim an honourable place in the queue for resurrection.

Left: The east window of Lincoln Cathedral reminds us that the impulse to tell the Christian story has always been a powerful one. The Garden of Eden, the serpent tempting Eve, the Flood, David and Goliath, then Bethlehem, the angels singing in the sky, the Passion and Gethsemane, the Crucifixion and the Day of Judgement. What a story! But simple people and often priests could not read, and if they could they did not understand Latin. So the story was told in pictures, using stained glass. This great craft developed alongside the great art of painting, but who knows the name of a single stained-glass worker? Yet these artist-craftsmen made glass whose rich and brilliant colour has never been matched, and the Sun shining through it gives us a feeling of warmth and comfort, a taste of Heaven which, as the poet George Herbert said: 'Is a great help to holiness.'

West of this sheep-rearing and wheat-growing country lies the county town of Lincoln, whose superb cathedral of honey-coloured stone is seen at its most dazzling by floodlight. The city itself, founded by the Romans in the first century AD as Lindum, was one of the strong points of their occupation. Linked by fine highways with York, Colchester and other centres, the Roman camp at Lindum played an important part in controlling the whole country.

Spread out before us around Lincoln is some of the world's finest rural scenery, the shires, embracing Northamptonshire and Leicestershire to the south and Nottinghamshire and Derbyshire to the west.

Northamptonshire is a county of 'squires and spires', so-called for its rural character, manor houses and parish churches with elegant spires. Leicestershire is great farming, hunting and cheese-making country. It is also rich in history. Near its western border lies Bosworth Field, site of one of the crucial battles of English history. Just as William the Conqueror settled once and for all the tribal feuding of Anglo-Saxon England, uniting the country under a ruthless monarch, so, by defeating Richard III at Bosworth, Henry Tudor settled once and for all the bitter emnity between the families of York and Lancaster. He founded the Tudor dynasty which took on the might of Spain and Rome, led the way to Elizabeth I, and so ushered in and presided over one of the most

Right: The Church of St Mary and All Saints stands by the River Nene at Fotheringhay, Northamptonshire. Here stood the castle, long since demolished, in whose banqueting hall Mary, Queen of Scots, was beheaded in 1587. A simple pen and ink sketch done on the spot shows the actual scene: the scaffolding in the middle and Mary with her little dog and two of her faithful waiting women, Mary Beeton and Mary Seaton standing by. When her head was off, her dog crept inside her petticoats and nuzzled against her knees.

Below: The Stoke Park Pavilions, near Stoke Bruerne, Northamptonshire, were designed by Inigo Jones (1573–1652), the leading architect of his day. He introduced into England the Palladian style, as in the beautiful Admiralty building in Whitehall, London, and the Banqueting Hall opposite, where Charles I spent the night before stepping out of the window onto the scaffold. Jones was also a fine stage designer, especially for performances at court which were a mixture of dialogue, dance and music, called masques. Many of his drawings for this part of his work still exist.

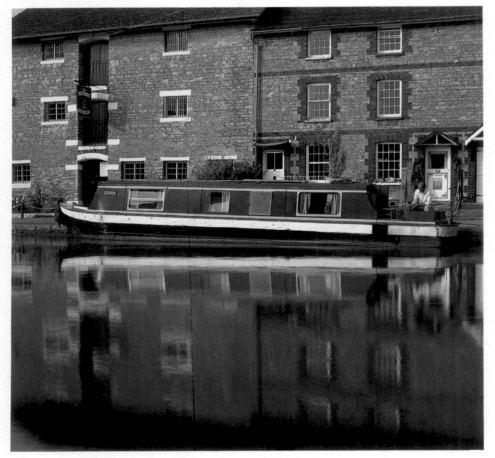

Above: Rockingham Castle, in northern Northamptonshire, is reputed to have been one of the first castles built by William the Conqueror, under his personal supervision, following the Battle of Hastings. The castle was built to help consolidate all the conquest to the South but by the end of the Middle Ages it had fallen into disrepair and Elizabeth I gave it to a gentleman, Edward Watson, who repaired and restored it. Charles Dickens often visited the castle, said to be Chesney Wold in his novel Bleak House.

Left: The Grand Union Canal runs through Stoke Bruerne, Northamptonshire. If you look at a map of Britain's ancient canal system, you will at once ask the question: 'But what happened to the villages and small towns in the way?' Naturally water was not taken around the houses. A canal was dug first and the streets and houses were built later. Barges were slow but sure, and non-polluting.

This flight of locks is on the Grand Union Canal at Foxton, Leicestershire. The canal system is one of Britain's greatest inventions. By an arrangement of steel gates operated from a canalside office, a series of basins can be flooded or emptied in turn until a barge is raised or lowered to a required level, a sort of liquid staircase enabling traffic to traverse the most difficult gradients. With the coming of steam and the internal combustion engine, the canals fell into disuse, but the shortage of energy is forcing governments to take a fresh look at them. They may move goods slowly, but they can carry vast loads with great reliability.

Fallow deer in Bradgate Park, Leicestershire, are a reminder that medieval Britain was heavily forested and the forests provided much of the country's food, including deer, wild boar, hare, pheasant, snipe, woodcock, wild duck and so on. But the nobility naturally wanted to preserve hunting rights for themselves, so rights of chase and trapping became one of the fiercest causes of hatred between the nobility and the peasantry. The art of poaching lies at the heart of the Robin Hood story. His band lived on what they could kill or trap and, if caught, were savagely punished. Most of Britain's forests have disappeared but there are still lanes with signs reading 'Beware of Deer' – in case you should run into one.

creative periods in British history. On Bosworth Field, the key unlocking Britain's astonishing future – constitutional, legal, scientific, commercial and artistic – was first turned and the floodgates opened.

Belvoir Castle, the ancestral home of the Dukes of Rutland in north-eastern Leicestershire, is also famous as the birthplace of a beautiful and gifted woman, Lady Diana Cooper, wife of the diplomat Duff Cooper (Earl of Norwich), who is a delightful writer, as her autobiographical volumes testify.

The glorious scenery in the Belvoir area is now threatened because it overlies the biggest coalfield in the British Isles. Such a store of natural wealth cannot be disregarded. The problem will doubtless be resolved by taking out the coal, filling in the huge cavities left behind, and re-landscaping the surface. The Coal Board and other mining interests are already adept at and committed to such conservationist measures, expensive though they may be.

Uppingham Church is in what used to be called Rutland until boundary changes eliminated this, the tiniest and one of the most beautiful of English counties. Now it is part of Leicestershire, which is great agricultural and great fox-hunting country, famous for its cheese, red Leicester being one of Britain's finest native varieties. Twelve miles (19 km) south of Leicester itself is Lutterworth where, between 1374 and 1384, John Wycliffe, the first man to translate the Bible from Latin into English, was rector. Despite the fact that such an act was heretical, he managed to die in his bed.

Nottingham Castle stands on a huge sandstone rock which is riddled with man-made caves. We always associated Nottingham with Robin Hood for, although he was almost certainly born in North Yorkshire, he and his Merry Men had most of their adventures in the forest land called Barnsdale, between Nottingham and South Yorkshire. Being outlaws their chief enemy was Nottingham's sheriff. Robin's name is first recorded at the beginning of the 13th century and the story of his prowess with bow and arrow gave great stimulus to its development as the deadly weapon it became over the following 300 years. All males above a certain age had to practice archery by law and the hitting power of the steel-tipped arrows was fearsome, especially when delivered in volleys and against unarmed horsemen.

Eastern Leicestershire, including Rutland, is one of the jewels of the British rural scene, with lovely stone-built villages, charming medieval churches and farms well stocked with beef and dairy cattle and sheep. Belvoir Castle in north-eastern Leicestershire and the Vale of Belvoir in which it is set is one of Britain's great beauty spots. Beneath it is one of the biggest coalfields in the country. So plans have been passed to plant a coal-mine there, but to fill in and restore the landscape afterwards, when it may look even more beautiful than it does now. If only we had known what we know now before we started on Durham, Staffordshire and South Wales!

Previous spread: *Wollaton Hall close by Nottingham University is a masterpiece of Elizabethan Renaissance architecture. It was built by the architect, Robert Smythson for Sir Francis Willoughby between 1580 and 1588, but it has belonged to the city of Nottingham since the 1920s. It houses the City of Nottingham Natural History Museum, and the Hall, its formal gardens and lovely park are open to the public throughout the year. Also near Nottingham is Newstead Abbey, which was built by Henry II in 1170 as penance for having ordered a group of retainers to rid him of that 'turbulent priest' (meaning Thomas à Becket), an order which they took literally, chopping him down in his own cathedral. When Henry VIII broke with Rome, the Abbey became the home of the Byron family, ancestors of the poet.*

Nottinghamshire is famous as the home ground of Robin Hood and his legendary band of outlaws who haunted the long stretch of forest called Barndale running northwards into Yorkshire, 'robbing the rich to give to the poor'. His story goes back a long way, the first mention of his name being in a manuscript dated about 1225. He and his 'merry men' are complementary to King Arthur and his knights. Robin has always fascinated me, and I had the great pleasure of writing *Robin Hood, His Life and Legend*, which a number of distinguished critics described as the best introduction to the Robin Hood story yet written.

North of the city of Nottingham, with its famous castle, are two magnificent buildings. First, the enchanting, cathedral-like Southwell Minster, built by the Normans between the 12th and 14th centuries. West of Southwell is Newstead Abbey, built in 1170 and later the home of the poet Lord Byron.

West of Nottingham lies Derby, a name known to lovers of luxury china the world over, to Edwardian housewives for a high quality, slow-burning domestic coal called Derby Brights, and to city gentlemen for a

Left: Buxton, Derbyshire, is an elegant spa town on the edge of the Peak District National Park, which is recognized as one of the scenically most stunning areas of Britain. The word spa *is the name of a town in Belgium where warm curative water was discovered in 1326 – to which invalids from all over Europe flocked for 600 years and more, until it ceased to be fashionable. But Roman soldiers serving in Britain had discovered such waters at least 1,200 years earlier. Bath, called* Aqua Sulis *by the Romans, Harrogate, Tunbridge Wells and other places were all known to have therapeutic springs which brought relief to the joints of soldiers who had to endure Britain's terrible winters.*

Below: Chatsworth, ancestral home of the Dukes of Devonshire, is one of the greatest of Britain's great houses. Built in 1707 for the first Duke, it has superb grounds laid out by the famous landscape gardener 'Capability' Brown who broke with the formal gardening tradition of the 16th and 17th centuries by developing a simple rearrangement of the landscape itself, using nature as his tutor. His style won great favour with the British nobility and if you could say that your garden had been 'done' by Capability Brown, you could hold your head up in the most select company. Brown was aided and abetted by another genius, Joseph Paxton, who built the Crystal Palace for the great 1851 Exhibition.

noble hat. But, to the world in general, Derby is renowned for the quietest, most reliable, most beautiful and most celebrated of all motor cars, the Rolls-Royce. Not only limousines are made here, but also jet engines which power many of the world's biggest aircraft.

Derbyshire contains many fascinating sights, including Chesterfield with its famous crooked-spired church, built with green timber which later warped. Then there are resorts, such as Matlock and Buxton. The Romans were familiar with the value of Buxton's springs, because Roman soldiers torn away from their Mediterranean sunshine and banished to the frozen wastes of northern England suffered cruelly from rheumatism and they wisely sought hot spa water to ease their pain. Buxton now has a beautiful little Opera House and mounts an annual festival of music and drama.

The crowning scenic glory of Derbyshire is the Peak District National Park, which occupies most of northern Derbyshire and extends into neighbouring counties. In the south of this unique area lie the limestone-lined Lathkill Dale and Dove Dale, both of which must come close to the top of Britain's beauty spots. My old Latin teacher, Lucy Cran, retired here, and I often called on her. At 87 years of age and blind, she was dependent upon a faithful black retriever who followed her every movement with his great liquid eyes, and who used to take her for walks. 'I call him Cicero,' she said. 'He's so much more civilized than most human beings. And so much more reliable.' Cicero brushed the carpet with his fine black tail in appreciation of the compliment.

For me the pride of the Peak District is Chatsworth, another of England's great houses and home of the Duke and Duchess of Devonshire. Its high reputation was confirmed by its famous 19th-century gardener, Joseph Paxton. He was the first to experiment with iron-framed structures filled with glass, using not only simple, plain surfaces, but also oval and semi-circular components specially manufactured to his design, the glass slotting into the iron frames which were made specially to fit. Here, among other plants, he grew giant water lilies from South America, with leaves of about 400 square inches (2,580 square centimetres), in artificial pools. Queen Victoria once visited Chatsworth with her latest three-month-old baby. To show the superlative weight-bearing quality of the leaves, Paxton asked if he might use the baby for a practical test. Placed gently in the middle of a single huge leaf, which sank a fraction of an inch and then steadied and stayed put, the baby was returned to her relieved mother, her petticoats bone-dry.

Rushup Edge, in the Peak District National Park, reveals what national parks are all about. Nature is not greedy, but she does like a goodly ration of fresh air and here in Derbyshire you feel you could walk to the horizon and hear her quietly breathing all the way. The farmhouse is squat and firmly planted against the weather, as is the barn in the distance, but both often have snow up to the eaves. And the modest tree has had its spine bent by some particularly fierce and persistent wind.

Paxton was later chosen as the designer of the Great Exhibition of 1851. He excelled himself with one of the most beautiful structures ever made by man, the famous Crystal Palace which unhappily burned down in 1936. When first erected, this sensational building posed one great problem. To avoid cutting down some trees, Paxton built the Palace around them. The trees attracted hordes of sparrows, which submitted visitors to a continuous shower of droppings. That great soldier the Duke of Wellington was finally called in by the Queen and asked for his advice. Without a moment's hesitation, he gave the solution. 'Try sparrowhawks, Ma'am,' he said. A pair of hawks was set free inside the great pleasure dome. Within a few hours, the droppings had ceased.

Left: Beresford Dale is one of the loveliest spots in the Peak District, the out-thrust southern end of the Pennine Chain. It is drained by the River Dove which gives its name to the most beautiful of all the Dales. When it comes to arguing about the rival claims of various British beauty spots, I believe you will always find the Peak District listed in the first half dozen and more often than not at the top. Magnificent hiking, camping, pony-trekking, climbing and pot-holing country is all within 20 miles (32 km) or so of Rochdale, Manchester, Stockport, Sheffield and other 'satanic mills'. Here on this vast base plate of limestone and shale capped with tough Millstone Grit, you really feel yourself in at the very birth of landscape, of the Earth's surface being wrenched into shape and of Mother Nature covering it up with a soft green blanket in order to hide the marks of that fearful struggle.

The Roaches near Leek in the Peak District National Park is a jumbled mass of hard rock known as Millstone Grit, much favoured by climbers. Millstone Grit used to be quarried in Nidderdale, close to where my wife was born.

The Peak District National Park is famed for its formidable mountain Kinder Scout; for Peveril Castle used by Sir Walter Scott in his novel Peveril of the Peak; for Hathersage, birthplace of Robin Hood's trusty mate Little John; for the southern end of the Pennine Way, conceived in the 1930s by Tom Stephenson, secretary of the Rambler's Association, and established by a group of ardent socialists – Barbara Castle, Richard Crossman, Hugh Dalton, and Harold Wilson; and the village of Eyam whose vicar persuaded his flock to stay rather than spread the infection when the plague hit them in 1665. Five out of every six died.

The Romans captured England, but they did not care to try conclusions with the savage Scots and Picts, especially on their own ground. So they built Hadrian's Wall right across northern England, with a mound and ditch along its northern side and small forts called milecastles at intervals along the south side. These milecastles, like the Cawfields one shown here, were living quarters for a hundred or so men who patrolled the top of the wall in shifts. To man the wall, the Romans used troops from Spain, Germany and the Middle East, men accustomed to warm, sunny weather. We can guess how they must have suffered because many skeletons examined by archaeologists have joints swollen by rheumatism. The wall was still intact when the Romans departed, but over the years locals have robbed it to build castles, churches, farmhouses and barns. It is remarkable how much of the original structure still remains above ground.

North-Eastern England

North-eastern England is where I taught after leaving Oxford University and where I met my wife Josephine. She was leading lady in the old Sheffield Repertory Theatre, the first theatre in which I worked, serving as designer, scene-painter and small-part actor. It is also where my daughter Bridget now lives with her family in North Yorkshire's Nidderdale. A region rich in personal associations, it also represents a panorama of British history and culture.

One of its most majestic features is Hadrian's Wall, which ran 73 miles (117 km) from Wallsend, near Newcastle upon Tyne, to Bowness, near Carlisle. This dramatic testimonial to Roman occupation, built in AD 123–128, has a mound and ditch along its northern side, also strong-points, some great and some small, planted at intervals from end to end. The smaller strong-points, called milecastles, were built to hold eight to thirty soldiers with their equipment, while the larger camps held about a thousand or more. The stone was quarried farther south and carried up to the site by soldiers with leather satchels slung over their shoulders like hikers' packs. This explains why all the stones are roughly the same size, and weigh between 15 to 20 pounds (7–9 kg), as much as a soldier could be expected to carry in a day's march. Building the wall must have been a dangerous and uncomfortable job, with the Picts and Scots slinging rocks from just out of range and screaming insults, all in the bitter cold of the Northumbrian winter – especially for men from warm Mediterranean lands.

Just south of the wall, below its eastern sector, is Vindolanda, a large rest-camp where the men went on leave after a spell on the wall. Here they could clean up, meet resident girlfriends, have their rheumatism treated, buy souvenirs and write letters home. Vindolanda is one of the most interesting Roman sites, including as it does

Whitby, North Yorkshire, is a seaside resort and fishing harbour, famous as the birthplace of Captain Cook, one of the greatest of all navigators, who charted vast stretches of the Australian and New Zealand coastlines before he was struck down in Tahiti. On the headland above the town stands the battered skeleton of the Abbey, site of the historic Synod where Gaelic and Romish Christianity came into conflict over the precise date of Easter and the correct haircut for monks. The Gaelic monks opted for a narrow strip across the head, while the Romish ones favoured the circle embracing the top of the head. In the end they agreed on the Romish way.

the complete foundation of its governor's official dwelling. More Roman writing has been found there than anywhere else in Europe, mostly lists and official orders inscribed on thin slivers of wood. Another interesting find was part of a centurion's purple tunic with gold thread running through it. Cut into squares, it was used in the ladies' toilet. The common soldiers used sponges which they washed and hung on nails for later use.

The North-east was frontier country for the Romans. But much has changed since those days, not just

98

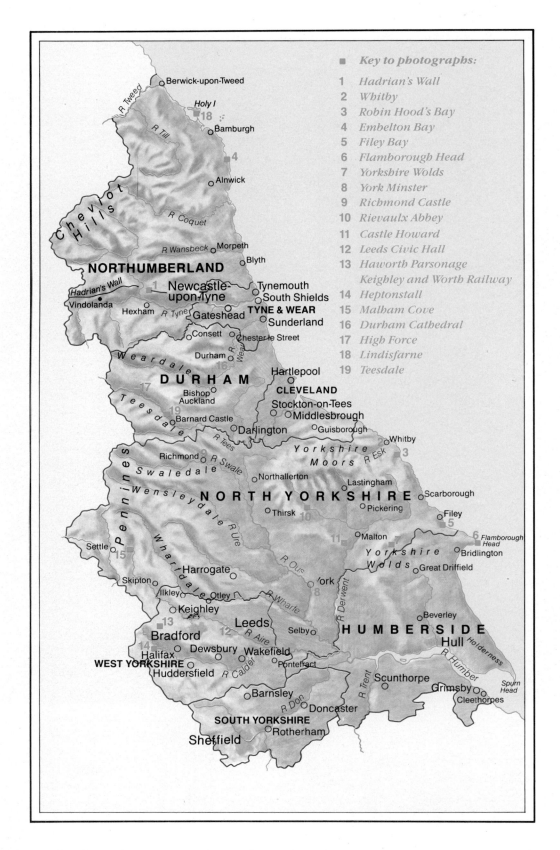

Key to photographs:
1   Hadrian's Wall
2   Whitby
3   Robin Hood's Bay
4   Embelton Bay
5   Filey Bay
6   Flamborough Head
7   Yorkshire Wolds
8   York Minster
9   Richmond Castle
10 Rievaulx Abbey
11 Castle Howard
12 Leeds Civic Hall
13 Haworth Parsonage
    Keighley and Worth Railway
14 Heptonstall
15 Malham Cove
16 Durham Cathedral
17 High Force
18 Lindisfarne
19 Teesdale

by human intervention but also from natural processes. For example, since Roman times, the sea has remorselessly bombarded the Holderness coast of Humberside and a strip of land 2 to 3 miles (3–5 km) wide has vanished beneath the sea, although some of the eroded rock has been used by the waves to build up Spurn Head.

North of Holderness is Filey, where I had my first job in a prep school on the cliffs, only a short distance from Scarborough. Filey was a revelation to me – that long sweep of golden sand with a rocky headland, Filey

Brigg, at the end, and the sea frets suddenly blotting out everything as if a veil were being drawn over a scene too enticing for human gaze.

North of Scarborough is the North York Moors National Park, which contains England's largest expanse of heather, a superb spectacle when in bloom in late summer. Coastal cliffs line much of the park in the east, where the lovely village of Whitby is situated. Here the immortal Captain James Cook received his baptism in seamanship and went on to become one of the world's greatest navigators before being killed in Hawaii, when only 50 years old.

Whitby is also famous in the history of the Church. In its famous Abbey, now a ruin perched on the cliffs, Celtic Christianity confronted Roman Christianity and, with the help of its Abbess Hilda, settled differences over

At Robin Hood's Bay we are reminded that the name Robin Hood appears all over Britain attached to lanes, fields, woodlands, farms, inns, and here to a most attractive coastal resort in North Yorkshire. Robin Hood exists, like King Arthur, outside the realm of recorded history, yet he is powerfully planted inside the mythology of medieval times. I believe that Robin Hood was a genuine folk hero who, in order to get closer to the red deer and kill them more easily, wore a red, woollen hood over his Lincoln green habit. And his connexion with Yorkshire? Perhaps one of his encounters was with a boat-load of pirates off the Yorkshire coast.

A flock of sheep are being driven around a headland at Embleton Bay, Northumberland, at low tide. They are on their way to being dipped, the trot along the sand obviously being shorter than trotting to the gate, along a lane, through another gate, past a farm where they keep a very unfriendly dog, and then across the main road and through yet another gate. Besides it is summer and the wet sand is cool to the feet. Northumberland has always been great sheep country.

the true date of Easter and monks' haircuts.

Inland, the North-east possesses some of Britain's noblest buildings. Beverley, north of Hull in Humberside, boasts a glorious cathedral with a pair of tall decorated Gothic towers, finely proportioned and exquisitely carved. Within it is the Frith Stool, or chair of peace for use in the sanctuary, half a century older than the church itself. Beverley is precious to the acting fraternity for it was here that the first stage miracle took place. Back in the 13th century a local company was performing one of the famous Mystery plays in front of the Minister. A small boy, unable to push his way to the front of the audience to get a decent view, clambered up the steps of the giant steeple to watch from above. The stones of the parapet gave way and he fell 300 feet (90 metres) to the ground. But instead of being dashed to

101

Flamborough Head is an excellent example of the sea at work on a chalk headland. Waves angled northwards and southwards by the changing tides and wind have worn away the headland on both sides, at length breaking through to form an arch. In the end, this arch will collapse, leaving an isolated pillar, called a stack, out to sea. Then the waves will get to work demolishing the stack which will become a hump visible only at low water. In the end it will disappear altogether and only very old gentlemen will tell you that they remember the days when it was there, and you will not believe them until they show you a photograph like this one.

When I left Oxford University, I spent a happy year teaching at a Filey school called Southcliffe, with the sea in front of it and the 13th hole of the Filey Golf Course in its back garden. Filey Bay, as shown here, is a magnificent curving stretch of clear sand backed by cliffs, with a low spur of rock called the Brigg guarding its northern end. I often walked north to Scarborough to visit my friend Eddy Vincent, the local doctor and an excellent amateur pianist. After tea with him and his mother, he played for an hour or so and he was the first to introduce me to Chopin, Beethoven, Schubert and the English madrigals, thus opening magical doors, which have remained open ever since. I left Filey to play the Second Messenger in Richard III at London's New Theatre for £4 a week and have never regretted it.

East and south of the Pennines are vast areas of Britain which are
tolerably flat and quick to claim a long and rich agricultural heritage. One
of these areas, long associated with sheep-rearing, is the rolling, low chalk
hills of the Yorkshire Wolds, shown here east of Malton. And east of the
Yorkshire Wolds, in what is now Humberside, are two of Britain's most
celebrated homes, Burton Agnes, near Bridlington, and Burton Constable,
near Kingston upon Hull. These homes are not stately in size, but more
than stately in their history and associations; both are examples as fine as
any in the kingdom of Tudor architecture at its very best.

103

Above: Richmond Castle, seen through the bridge, guards
the Vale of York. It is one of Britain's oldest castles with
some of its 11th-century stonework still surviving and,
despite its age, its shape and layout are still plain. Until
1962 it was the most important object in the town. But
then the old Richmond Theatre was discovered. Built in
1799 and used for decades as a furniture store, it had
formerly been part of the theatre circuit based on York and
run by a celebrated actor-manager named Tate Wilkinson.

But it had fallen into disuse and had finally been
abandoned. It has now been restored and brought back to
its former glory as one of Europe's most beautiful old
theatres.

Above right: York Minster, seat of Britain's second
archbishop and one of the half dozen miracles of medieval
stonework, was begun in 1220 and continued through the
next two and a half centuries. It is one of the most
exhilarating repair and construction jobs ever performed.
For half a century it was in danger of collapsing under the
vibration from traffic and the explosion of German bombs.

But surveyor Bernard Fielden and a team of brilliant
colleagues evolved a plan for underpinning the whole
structure with a huge raft of concrete supported by groynes,
the spaces between them forming a perfect place for a
subterranean museum displaying York's long and eventful
history, particularly in Viking times; for along with
Dublin, York was one of the leading Viking settlements
outside Scandinavia.

pieces he floated down safe and sound and, for his devotion to the art of acting, was given a front seat for the rest of the performance.

While on the subject, I must mention Richmond in North Yorkshire, whose genuine 18th-century theatre, a 200-seater in full working order, is one of the finest and oldest in Europe. In the late 18th and early 19th centuries, it was one of the circuit of small playhouses based on

York and most of the great performers of the day appeared there, including David Garrick, Sarah Siddons and Edmund Kean. But it had long fallen into decline and was being used as a furniture store when it was discovered during the Second World War. In the early 1960s, when it was restored to its former glory, I appeared there in my One-Man Show to a full and appreciative house!

But the most famous building in the North-east is York Minster, one of the glories of European Gothic architecture, with its own Archbishop, second only to Canterbury's, and then only because an earlier Archbishop of Canterbury was taller and heavier. You see, no

Left: By the end of the Middle Ages there was an abbey, monastery or convent only a few miles away in any direction, such was the power and influence of the Church, and the 400 years between 1066 and 1500 saw the flowering of great church architecture. Many of its finest examples can be seen in North-east England as here at Rievaulx and also at Bolton, Byland, Fountains, Jervaulx and Rosedale. Most of these jewels now lie in ruins, but when set in glorious landscapes they are probably more compelling than the originals ever were. The monastic life was far from a lazy one, for it laid the foundations of the woollen industry, which put Britain in the vanguard of the Industrial Revolution. Sir Harold Wilson showed a fine sense of history in choosing Rievaulx for his title when he entered the House of Lords.

Above: Castle Howard, North Yorkshire, is the most magnificent of Britain's great houses. It was designed by Sir John Vanbrugh, who was also a major dramatist, for the Earl of Carlisle at the very end of the 17th century. Touring this great mansion, with its long gallery and famous collection of British costumes, we are driven to wonder what kind of person would need such a vast edifice. The answer can only be to confirm the owner's wealth and importance, to justify his titles and decorations.

Visiting such places, one can only admire the resourcefulness of those families who out-manoeuvred Britain's excruciating tax system by moving into a small corner of their great homes and letting 'the common herd' or 'lower orders' (phrases known only in Britain) enjoy their ancestral mansions for £2 a head (children half price), or by turning their estates into safari parks or, as my old friend Edward Montagu has done, into the world's greatest motor museum.

Haworth Parsonage was the home of the three Brontë sisters, Emily, Charlotte and Anne, who lived there along with their dissolute brother Branwell, from the 1820s to the 1840s. And it was here, surrounded by a wild and forbidding landscape, that they dreamed of becoming novelists and went on to put their dreams into practice. The house contains most of its original furnishings which were touched and used by these gifted girls. In your imagination you can join them in their daily round, walking with them to Top Withens, prototype of Wuthering Heights, and shielding their drunken brother from his father's wrath – and writing, writing, always writing.

one had decided which of the Archbishops was the more important, and so, during a visit from the Papal Legate in 1176, the two prelates fought it out with bare fists in the actual cathedral. The Archbishop of Canterbury knocked York down and sat on the Legate's right hand himself. York, recovering his senses, scrambled to his feet and sat down in Canterbury's lap. It was left to the King to bind them both over to keep the peace for five years. Such scenes do not happen today, except occasionally in London's Downing Street, where Cabinet Ministers, disagreeing over some point of policy, have been known to come to fisticuffs and even to break up furniture.

York Minster, which was built between 1220 and 1470, was in danger of falling down until, in 1959, it was rescued with a vast underpinning of concrete, a huge

unsinkable raft full of cavities which are now used as a museum celebrating York's long and glorious history. For York had been a fine Roman city called Eboracum, and after Roman times it was one of the biggest and busiest Viking settlements in Europe, a fact only recently brought to light by modern archaeology.

The North-east has too many wonderful things to see, but not to be missed are the ruins of Fountains and Rievaulx Abbeys and two famous stately homes – Sir John Vanbrugh's Castle Howard and Harewood House, home of the Earl of Harewood, the Abbeydale Industrial Hamlet near Sheffield, which recalls Yorkshire's industrial past, the Keighley and Worth Railway, a heartwarming reminder of the great days of steam, and Haworth, home of the Brontë sisters, the third most popular tourist attraction in England after Stratford-

The Keighley and Worth Valley Railway, West Yorkshire, is one of the 30 odd fragments of standard and narrow gauge lines rescued by amateur enthusiasts from the contraction of Britain's unique web of railways in the 1950s and 1960s. It represents the typical British lunacy for collecting fragments of their own history and either putting them in museums, or on their sitting-room mantelpieces, or, as in this case, bringing them back into service. Kent and the South Coast, the Midlands, Wales, Yorkshire and North Lancashire all boast splendid examples of rescued railways, and even the north of Scotland has a very fine one.

109

Above: Heptonstall in West Yorkshire, like so many of the loveliest villages in the North-east, is set in (or rather on the top of) magnificent moorland about 10 miles (16 km) west of the city of Bradford. Here you can see the simple cottages lived in by early weavers and savour the textile trade when it was in its infancy, before power looms had been dreamed of.

Right: As Manchester's Free Trade Hall expresses cotton, so the Civic Hall of Leeds expresses wool in all its manifestations. The Civic Hall marks the assurance, confidence and pride of a great city certain of its origins and secure in its future. The wool trade was rooted in great monastic foundations and was for centuries the staple industry of Britain. The dead were by law buried not in coffins but in woollen shrouds; dire penalties were inflicted on those who failed to follow this practice. One of the most talked-of spectacles in the late 18th century was the shearing of a chosen sheep and the turning of its wool into a complete suit of clothes within 12 hours. All the processes (including dyeing) were carried out within the allotted time before thousands of onlookers as if it had been the Highland Games or the Cup Final. Engravings of the scene were made and sold throughout the kingdom.

110

upon-Avon and the Lake District. But for me (we all have preferences), the Saxon crypt at Lastingham, north-west of Pickering, is the most moving. Among sites of scenic grandeur are the waterfalls at Aysgarth in Wensleydale and High Force, England's highest waterfall, in Durham.

Another face of the North-east is exemplified by the great cities of Leeds and Bradford, once world centres of the woollen industry, and Sheffield, a name synonymous with steel. Though they are not everyone's idea of beautiful places, both are within easy reach of some of Britain's most haunting scenery, namely that backbone of northern England, the Pennine Chain.

The Pennine Way, a cross-country route for experienced hikers, extends from Derbyshire's Peak District, through the Yorkshire Dales National Park, with its exquisite, sheltered valleys and impressive

At Malham Cove is a limestone cliff 240 feet (73 metres) high. Malham Beck once tumbled down in a waterfall, and so into the River Aire. But now it flows through the limestone, bubbling to the surface at the base of the cliff. The southern part of the Yorkshire Dales National Park is so rich in natural and man-made beauty that it is difficult to make a creditable selection. But if you see Malham Tarn, Kilnsey Crags, Gordale Scar, the medieval field system at Grassington, Kettlewell, Hubberholme, Arncliffe and Bolton Abbey you will have seen some of the finest that Britain has to offer – all of it within a single day's vigorous walking.

The Yorkshire Dales National Park is a lovely place, but I am a bit prejudiced about Yorkshire. It was where I got my first job and where I met my wife. Indeed I can speak with a little bit of a Yorkshire accent, not very successfully I fear, but good enough to pass muster in the South – and I am improving. The Pennine Chain runs like a spine down the centre of northern England. The region is marked by miles upon miles of dry-stone walling built with tremendous skill and blinding hard work. The hills are honeycombed not only with natural caves, but also with old lead workings. Indeed lead was worked in Greenhow above Pateley Bridge in the first century after Christ.

limestone and sandstone (Millstone Grit) landscapes, to the Northumberland National Park, which includes the lovely Cheviot Hills, a volcanic outcrop north of Hadrian's Wall.

A delight for those who love remote places, punctuated by peaceful sandy bays, old castles and charming fishing villages, is the Northumberland coast. This region includes Lindisfarne, or Holy Island. It was here that a local lad named Cuthbert came to join one of England's earliest monasteries. He was so fine a Christian and so beloved of his fellow monks that they chose him to be their prior. His fame spread throughout northern England. But after he died in AD 687, the Vikings made a terrible raid on Lindisfarne, slaughtering many of the monks and burning parts of the Abbey. The survivors decided to leave the island, taking with them the body of

113

Above: High Force in upper Teesdale, just below Langdon Beck, is one of the most spectacular waterfalls in Britain, tumbling 70 feet (21 metres) down from the moors over the Great Whin Sill – a sharp ridge made of tough rock which was forced upwards in a molten state through the existing rocks. All this happened millions of years ago, but the waterfall testifies to the hardness of the rock. You would think that such a weight of falling water would be hard to stop, but in bitterly cold weather it actually freezes and the thunder of its waters is stilled.

Left: Lindisfarne, largest of the Farne Islands off the coast of Northumberland, is joined to the mainland by a causeway, passable only at a low tide. The Priory shown here replaced one built in the seventh century and destroyed by Vikings around AD 800. St Cuthbert was Prior of the early one. It was here that he died and from here his devoted followers, fleeing from Viking raiders, carried his coffin until, more than 200 years later, they laid it to rest in Durham. The Northumberland coast with its low beaches and shelving sands was perilously open to attack by Norsemen and the abbies and priories in the North-east yielded a store of treasure, tempting the invaders to make deeper forays, finally leading to the building of their own capital city at York, which has yielded priceless evidence of their way of life in the ninth and tenth centuries.

115

their precious Cuthbert in an oaken coffin. But northern England was still mainly heathen. The precious burden was moved from place to place for more than 200 years until, one morning, after the monks had slept and prayed around the coffin, they awoke to find that it had moved a little way eastwards. The same thing happened night after night until they realized that Cuthbert's body inside the coffin was leading them to the great rock at Durham. There they carried it and there they started to build a new monastery which is now Durham Cathedral, one of the most magnificent in the world. The final resting place of the beloved Saint Cuthbert is behind the high altar. You can still see part of the coffin in which the monks carried him for all those years, also his richly embroidered cloak. Later a special Chapel was built in the cathedral, where they buried the Venerable Bede, the first English historian to whose writings we owe so much of the story of our island home.

Because Yorkshire has the Pennine Chain running through it, in many places more than 2,000 feet (610 metres) high, some people have the idea that it is a cold and inhospitable county. But where there are mountains, there are also sheltered valleys like Teesdale, into which soft upland soil has been washed to form rich lowland, and here you will find fields of buttercups as thick as any found in the South. Teesdale, Airedale, Wensleydale and Swaledale boast some of the finest farming country in the land, some of the most beautiful villages and some of the most magnificent monasteries.

116

Durham Cathedral, the most massive of British cathedrals, stands on a rock girdled by the River Wear. Perhaps because its builders were too earthbound, too well aware that it might, at any moment, have to serve as a stronghold, the cathedral does not aspire, but rather shows a powerful defensive aspect. But what glories are within to show the gentler and more sky-climbing face of Christianity: the coffin of St Cuthbert, the Chapel of Nine Altars and the Galilee Chapel, containing the remains of the Venerable Bede, who wrote the first History of England back in the eighth century.

The Solway Firth is an inlet of the Irish Sea separating northern Cumbria from a part of the Scottish mainland which is largely unspoiled because it doesn't go anywhere (forgive me Lowland Scots!), except to the Stranraer ferry. The trains which run down from Glasgow turn left at Dumfries and go belting on to London. But this part of Scotland boasts some of Britain's loveliest countryside. I find it particularly heart-warming because my mother was born in a hamlet called Glenlochar, just west of Castle Douglas. A few years ago I paid Glenlochar a visit. I asked the headmistress at the schoolhouse if I could see the classroom where my mother was educated nearly a hundred years earlier. She made me welcome but was unable to find my mother's name in the old school registers, most of which had been destroyed. But I was proud and happy to have confirmed my Scottishness by this simple act of piety.

North-Western England

Hadrian's Wall ended at Bowness-on-Solway hard by Carlisle in what is now northern Cumbria. Behind the Wall the Roman legions thought themselves more or less secure. But it has been suggested that this was not all of the story. The Romans were well equipped and generously provisioned with their rest camp at Vindolanda only a few miles away in what is now Northumberland. Among the infantry manning the Wall were three wings of cavalry, one from the Middle East, one from Spain and one from Germany, each wing being 600 strong. The horses needed oats. On the far side of the Wall were the Picts and Scots, who distilled a wondrous liquor known as whisky, and whose staple food was oatmeal. If you had been a Pict or a Scot, imagine what you could get in exchange for a supply of oats and whisky! Was there then some trade going on between the adversaries? It is well known that Roman Britain did not fall by direct conquest but by a process of infiltration. The Romans employed Saxon mercenaries to help them hold off Saxon invaders. In the North, doubtless, there were some similar fraternal arrangements, especially at the two ends of the Wall.

For nearly 1,400 years after the Roman legions were called home and most of the Wall had collapsed, there was continuing warfare in the North. Nor did it abate as the Scots moved remorselessly from tribalism to a glorious nationhood. Raid followed raid into detested England, with killing, burning and looting. The raiders' favourite route was down through the North-west where the lakes and mountains invited them to pursue their chosen art of guerrilla warfare instead of facing the hazards of pitched battle.

For centuries Carlisle suffered all the to and fro of bloodshed and became the bastion and bulwark protecting England from its fearsome neighbours. The ruins of its castle bear witness to the long struggle. Finally

119

Top: Gypsies water their horses in the River Eden at Appleby, Cumbria, where they have come from all over England and Wales to mount the yearly fair. In 1806 the great actor George Frederick Cooke was caught and imprisoned in Appleby after failing to pay for his week's lodging in Manchester. The manager of the Glasgow Theatre where he was due to appear the following week managed to secure his release by sending him a couple of weeks salary in advance! My old friend Finlay Currie, who played the convict Magwitch in David Lean's fine film Great Expectations, ran an antiquarian book business from here.

Above: Dora's Field at Rydal, Cumbria, was bought and planted with daffodils by William Wordsworth for his daughter's birthday a century and a half ago. It is now under the guardianship of the National Trust. Wordsworth and his enchanting sister Dorothy, along with Coleridge and Thomas de Quincy, form one of the great watersheds in the history of British poetry. Reared under the powerful spell of Britain's unique satiric tradition and the iron bonds of the heroic couplet, they sought to bring poetry back under the wing of nature. At Grasmere and Rydal you can see their homes and the landscapes that captured their imagination.

ISLE OF MAN

CUMBRIA

Solway Firth

Hadrian's Wall

Carlisle

Maryport
Workington
Whitehaven

Bassenthwaite
Lake
Derwent Water
Keswick
Cumbrian Mts
Lake
Scafell Pikes
District
Coniston
Water
Grasmere
Ambleside
Windermere
Kendal

Penrith
R. Eden
Appleby
Brough
Ullswater
Haweswater

Douglas

Dalton
Barrow-in-Furness
Morecambe
Lancaster
Bowland
Forest

R. Kent
Kirkby Lonsdale
R. Lune

LANCASHIRE

Blackpool
Preston
Blackburn

Clitheroe
Colne
R. Ribble
Burnley

Southport
Formby

Bolton
Wigan
St Helens

Bury
Rochdale
Oldham

GREATER
MANCHESTER
Manchester
Altrincham
Warrington
Widnes

Ashton-under-Lyme
Stockport

Liverpool
Birkenhead
MERSEYSIDE
Wirral
R. Mersey

Macclesfield

Chester

CHESHIRE
Crewe

R. Dee

Key to photographs:
1 Solway Firth
2 Appleby
3 Dora's Field, Rydal
4 Yew Tree Tarn
5 High Cup Nick
6 Striding Edge, Helvellyn
7 Gleaners, near Lazonby
8 Sunbiggin Tarn
9 Langdale Pikes
10 Aira Force
11 Stonethwaite Beck
12 Ullswater and Hallin Fell
13 Port St Mary
14 Blackpool
15 Manchester
16 Formby Sands
17 Liverpool Cathedral
18 Gawsworth Hall
19 Jodrell Bank

came the Jacobite Rebellion of 1745 when a single Highlander, the last remnant of the invading forces which had reached as far south as Derby, marched through the city defiantly playing his pipes. The Scots then more or less called it a day.

Two of the wonders of north-western England are the 12th-century Lanercost Priory, north-east of Carlisle, a kind of sister-ruin to magical Brinkburn Priory over in Northumberland, and the beautiful, fertile Vale of Eden. A tributary of the River Eden, the Eamont, rises in the

121

majestic Lake Ullswater in that demi-paradise, that 'other Eden' of which my refugee friend spoke in the first few lines of my introduction to this book. This is the Lake District, England's biggest National Park and one of the most beautiful, largely because it cradles vast stretches of water among its hills and mountains. As an island people, who happen also to be inveterate gardeners, the British respond to such a mixture with an unquenchable appetite.

Sixty or seventy years ago, children were taught to memorize 'the bays and capes of England', the location of the most famous lighthouses and the names of the highest mountains. I remember one rhyme which ended with the mysterious words: 'Scafell, Helvellyn, Skiddaw, Saddleback'. And here they all are, as large as life and twice as handsome – a bunch of the highest mountains in the land separated by precipitous valleys carved out by glaciers thousands of years ago, and finally filled with limpid, ice-cold water as the glaciers melted.

Yew Tree Tarn is a beautiful artificial lake near Coniston. Close by Coniston is Brantwood, home of John Ruskin, artist, critic and prophet, who was the first to proclaim the genius of Britain's greatest painter Turner, and who also saw the dangers and disasters that lay ahead if mankind failed to curb his greed and rejected the notion of universal brotherhood. He was one of the greatest of all Englishmen. At Brantwood you can see some of his paintings, his simple, homespun cloths, and the large, heavy boots in which he tramped through this glorious landscape.

Above: The Great Whin Sill at High Cup Nick is part of a structure which runs from Lindisfarne right across the north of England to Cumbria. My wife and I were taken to the Sill a few years ago by my friends John McMillan and Leslie Turnbull, well-known Northumbrian historians, and we found a small piece of local amethyst which we had made into a brooch.

Left: The combine harvester has done its job. But if you have time and patience and a few chickens in your back garden, there is enough corn left on the ground to feed them for a fortnight. When I was a small boy, village women used to do this vital job of gleaning and small boys and girls were allowed to stay away from school and lend a hand to their white-aproned, sun-bonneted mothers, as I myself did.

123

Here natural formations, clothed with torrents of green, subject to ever-changing weather and lit by ever-changing light, stop the heart with their loveliness. But people come to the Lake District not only for the scenery, but also for the poets who have celebrated it with some of the most moving writing in the English language, especially William Wordsworth and his lovely sister

From Blea Tarn in Cumbria there is a fine view of Langdale Pikes. As you can imagine, rivers of ice crawling remorselessly over the countryside have the effect of both deepening valleys and smoothing the rocks, grinding off the rough edges. But Langdale Pikes offers a rougher aspect because its jagged scars and ridges were formed from resistant volcanic rocks which were thrust upwards about 450 million years ago. In the foreground, the mountain tarn, fed by rain and snow melting down the sides of the surrounding rocks, occupies a basin scoured out by some long-vanished glacier.

Left: The problem with trying to describe a complex landscape like the Lake District is one of time-scale. The oldest rocks, the Skiddaw slates, began to form in a shallow sea more than 500 million years ago. The Borrowdale volcanics in the central fells were erupted 450 million years ago, while the south contains rocks which formed slowly from sediments about 300 million years ago. Around the Lake District are somewhat more recent limestones and sandstones. And then, one million years ago (only yesterday in Earth time) came the Ice Age. Thus the basic landscape of the Lake District consists of deep-trenched valleys gouged out by glaciers moving remorselessly downwards, leaving here and there isolated hollows on the slopes. As the glaciers melted, pure limpid water filled the floors of these mountain lakes. Lakeland is full of them and Sunbiggin Tarn in this picture is one of its loveliest.

125

Aira Force, above Ullswater in the north-eastern part of the Lake District, is a 70-foot (21-metre) high waterfall. It is winter and all the speed and power of the water has been overwhelmed by the frost and ice. Northern England, and especially the north-west, has many words taken over from the various peoples who invaded Britain in the early days of its history, for example, beck, Scandinavian for brook, tarn, another Norse word for a mountain lake, and force (or fors) an Old Norse word for waterfall. Our language is even more mixed than our blood!

126

The exquisite Stonethwaite Beck in Borrowdale, Cumbria, may lead people
to think of the Lake District only as a place of beauty. But others see each
rock, each peak as a challenge to their skill, muscle and daring. On the
western side of Cumbria there lives a sheep farmer who has been called the
world's greatest athlete by the Olympic runner Chris Brasher. His name is
Joss Naylor. Born in 1936 he holds the record for winning the 23-mile (37-
km) up-hill and down-dale Ennerdale mountain race nine times between
1968 and 1977. Try that for a jog!

This picture of Ullswater and Hallin Fell in the Lake District reminds me
of a dream from which I thought I should never wake up. I was in a house
with many rooms and there was a lovely girl in each room and I would
win a prize if I chose the loveliest one. So I moved from room to room and
each girl seemed lovelier than the last, and when I had seen them all I
found that I couldn't make a choice. So I asked if I could go through the
rooms again, but still I couldn't choose. The man in charge let me go on
trying until in the end I chose them all. As if he foresaw that one day his
beloved Lake District would belong officially to the nation, Wordsworth
described it as 'a sort of National Property in which every man has a
right and interest who has an eye to perceive and a heart to enjoy'.

128

Striding Edge, Helvellyn, is striking testimony to the fact that the whole Lake District was shaped in the recent Ice Age by glaciers, those huge rivers of ice that crawled downhill from the mountains, scraping a deep pathway as they moved. Here two glaciers approached one another back to back, each one carving its own path until all that divided them was this long, sharp edge. Striding Edge is one of the most dramatic and unexpected features in the Lake District, the biggest of Britain's National Parks.

Dorothy, Thomas de Quincy and Samuel Taylor Coleridge. At Grasmere, near the centre of the Lake District, is Dove Cottage where the Wordsworths lived from 1799 to 1808, writing and entertaining their friends. We walk into it, upstairs and down, seeing the little bedroom where Coleridge slept, and below stairs we find the tiny kitchen with its stone floor, its copper, its pots and pans – just as it was when those exquisite minds thronged it. We imagine Wordsworth 'a clergery looking

gentleman' sitting down one evening to leaf through his beloved sister's daily journal and putting into poetry what she had just noted in prose.

'I wandered lonely as a cloud
That floats on high o'er vales and hills
When all at once I saw a crowd
A host of golden daffodils.'

It is easy to imagine Coleridge, racked with perpetual fever, talking long into the night, trying to harness the fiery horses of his mind into a single, all-embracing chariot. And when de Quincy arrives, do we not detect a faint whiff of opium? And can we imagine the six-day coach trip to London and six days coming back?

West of Cumbria, in the Irish Sea, is the Isle of Man, which in Viking times was the headquarters of the Lord of all the Isles to the West of Scotland. It preserves to this day the primitive parliament called the House of Keys with which the Norsemen ruled their kingdoms. Here

Port St Mary is on the south coast of the Isle of Man. In Viking times the islands around the western coast of Scotland were controlled by a chieftain called the Lord of the Isles who ruled his domain with a rough and ready assembly called the Tynwald. This parliament still functions. The Isle of Man has some fine agricultural country and an alluring, unspoiled coastline offering a choice of high cliffs and sandy beaches. My old friend Bill Naughton, author of Alfie All in Good Time and other plays, lives on the island. It was our cherished ambition to launch an appeal for the repair of the magnificent St Magnus cathedral at Peel. If the inhabitants do not beat us to it, one day we may attempt it!

Blackpool is a sort of innocent Vanity Fair, a holiday haunt for Northern England's peerless working-classes. The Tower, 518 feet (158 metres) high, is an imitation of the Eiffel Tower in Paris. When all the lights are turned on and the sound systems are in top gear, Blackpool looks and sounds as if not only the visitors but the houses, hotels, the esplanade and side streets are all dancing and having a 'right good time'. For me Blackpool is loveliest when the beaches are empty, the summer mess has been cleared up and you can sit and read in a glass-screened shelter in perfect peace.

once a year are mounted the Tourist Trophy motorcycle races when riders from the world compete with each other going flat out – and they are indeed nearly flat as they take those fearsome corners almost scraping their knees. At Laxey on this attractive island is the world's biggest water-wheel, which began to operate in 1854, and we ought not to forget that the crew of Lord Nelson's *Victory* at the Battle of Trafalgar in 1805 boasted a single proud Manxman.

South of Cumbria are Lancashire with its string of famous coastal resorts, including Blackpool with its glittering autumn illuminations, and the great industrial conurbations of Merseyside and Greater Manchester.

The city of Manchester was formerly the richest in Europe and it even astounded London with its energy, its initiative, its wealth and its creative power. Here the Industrial Revolution grew to its peak on a diet of steam and coal, inventive brains and cotton, which was turned

131

Above: You would not believe that where the high-rise and factory buildings now stand in Manchester, there were once cottages full of men and women occupied day and night spinning cotton and making some of the most delicate fabrics ever made, waiting unawares for the advent of the Spinning Jenny and the power loom which were to put the whole cottage industry out of business, draw thousands of new workers to the area and establish Manchester as Europe's richest city. Nor did they realize that Manchester would later be hit by an even bigger revolution wrought by the invention of synthetic threads. But Manchester is still one of Britain's half dozen greatest cities, bustling with financial and artistic life, now especially renowned for having transformed its famous Cotton Exchange into one of the most adventurous and prestigious theatres in the land.

Right: Large stretches of Britain's coasts are being eaten away by the sea, as on the east coast of England where whole villages once bursting with life now lie under the waves. Indeed it is said that you can sometimes hear the bells of long-drowned churches still ringing. Here on the 7-mile (11-km) stretch of Formby coast in Lancashire below Southport, the opposite is happening as the sea retreats and is replaced by sand. This process has continued so that the one-time fishing village of Formby is now some way inland and the coast has become a stretch of sand dunes, partially controlled by thick hummocks of coarse grass and carefully spaced out pine trees, in order to prevent the situation from getting out of hand.

132

Left: Below the Lantern of Liverpool's Roman Catholic Cathedral is a circular building. The Service, the place from which the priest serves the bread and wine to sinful mankind (like a gentle but well-trained butler) is in the centre, with mankind wrapped around him like a warming blanket – just as people wrapped themselves around Jesus in Galilee 2,000 years ago, seeking His healing touch. This break with tradition of priest and congregation confronting each other is one of the great religious and architectural inspirations of our time. I love genuine cities but always set the noisy, bustling, power-house types, such as Glasgow and Liverpool, above the quiet, respectable, well-groomed ones. When Dr Johnson was travelling from London to Salisbury he ventured to ask the coachman what kind of a city Salisbury was. The coachman, doubtless exaggerating, replied: 'Debauched sir, like all cathedral cities.'

Gawsworth Hall, near Macclesfield in Cheshire, is a typical oak-framed manor house built around 1475. It is basically a timber framework with much sophisticated jointing, filled in with plaster, probably made of cow-dung mixed with sand, with chopped horse-hair stirred in to hold it together more strongly. My wife and I went to buy a home in Buckinghamshire some years ago. The owner, a local farmer, showed us over one particularly pleasant property, pointing out with special pride the corner beams supposedly supporting the ceiling. When we remarked on them, he pulled out a couple of oak pegs and showed that they were thin slivers of oak supporting nothing. He was quite unabashed, excusing himself by saying: 'The quality always likes a few beams about.' And when we asked him the name of the architect, he replied: 'We builds them first and architects them afterwards.'

into pure gold by the flying shuttles, power looms, spinning jennies and a score of other brilliant devices. In the mighty Free Trade Hall, the root, leaf, stem and flower of that precious plant are celebrated on the walls, tiles, columns and bannisters, in stained glass windows and table-cloths. All is cotton. The toll of life and limb and human suffering in the Industrial Revolution is not to be described. Tiny orphans, eight to ten years old and even younger, could be bought in and around London for ten shillings (50 pence) apiece and then taken north in bargeloads to crawl under the machines and gather up the precious cotton waste. But out of all this horror came millions of miles of the most delicate fabrics ever made, to adorn the royalty, nobility and bourgeoisie of Britain and mainland Europe.

In gentler times Manchester was renowned for acts of high culture and human betterment like the John Rylands Library, one of the finest in Europe, the Hallé Orchestra and Miss Horniman's famous Gaiety Theatre, the Opera House, the biggest theatre in England, and Sherratt and Hughes Bookshop. On a more terrible

testing ground, we recall the Lancashire Fusiliers who won glory at the Dardanelles with 'four VC's before breakfast'. Today there are two famed soccer teams, Manchester United and Manchester City, vying with each other and the great Liverpool and Everton in Merseyside for a place at the top of the League table and the intoxicating roar of the crowd.

So great and powerful was landlocked Manchester that it had to fashion itself a gateway into the outside world. The Manchester Ship Canal was an engineering wonder in an age of wonders, able to bring ocean-going ships from Liverpool into the heart of the city with raw materials, and out again with finished products.

South of Manchester is Cheshire, with its ancient walled county town of Chester and, south of Knutsford, the 'Cranford' of Mrs Gaskell, is Jodrell Bank, where we take a great leap into the world of modern astronomy. Here is a huge metal dish, the world's first radio telescope, which can be aimed at any part of the heavens to collect the constant stream of signals pouring out from the stars towards our tiny spaceship Earth.

Jodrell Bank, in Cheshire, is famous for its huge radio telescope. During the Second World War scientists working with sophisticated electronic equipment began to pick up signals from outer space, and it soon became clear that the heavens were alive with radio impulses from many unsuspected sources millions of light years away, pouring out vast quantities of energy. In other words the sky was flooded with activity hitherto undreamed of. A fresh kind of telescope was needed to investigate these phenomena. The new telescopes consisted of a large metal dish, such as this one designed by the famous astronomer Sir Bernard Lovell, which could scan great areas of the skies in the northern hemisphere and record what exists in them. Astronomy had taken a new and exciting turn. It had outgrown the capacity of the human eye. It had come of age.

135

The relics of industry often add a touch of mystery and even nobility to a rural scene like this one near Dudley in the West Midlands. Haystacks lining the river, which winds away into the distance, and the chimney with its attendant house add a valuable depth to the scene and also a touch of melancholy, especially as winter is on its way. Ruin and dereliction are important elements in a landscape, making us grieve as well as rejoice. As D H Lawrence wrote: 'I weep like a child for the past.' In the 1930s my brother taught mathematics at Dudley Grammar School and our aunt was an elementary school teacher for 54 years at Bilston, Willenhall and other Midland centres. So I have a great affection for this area.

The Heart of England

At the heart of England lies the Black Country, so-called because the smoke and grime of Birmingham, its great capital city, was so overpowering and the accent of its people so blazingly forthright. And yet this fearsome industrial area is surrounded by places of surpassing grace and beauty; it is like a lump of coal set in a diamond tiara.

For example, north of Birmingham is Cannock Chase, an ancient hunting ground rich in superb woodland, and northwards again is the Trent and Mersey Canal leading away towards Liverpool. How can I describe the romance of England's canal system, those friendly waterways so cunningly fashioned of puddled clay, with their stair-cases of locks to take the water up hill and down dale, and their mighty horses pulling the barges slowly and surely along the tow-paths? They fell victims to the rush of industry and faster forms of travel, and are now used mainly by holiday-makers who seek quiet and peaceful journeys through a rural paradise. But they played a vital role in the development of industrial Britain. They were the humble carriers of Britain's wealth and commercial prosperity. For example, the Trent and Mersey Canal passes through Stoke-on-Trent, centre of the Potteries where some of the finest British chinaware was created. And still is.

East of Cannock Chase is the ancient and historic town of Lichfield, famous for its unique, 'triple-spired' cathedral, but even more famous as the birthplace of Samuel Johnson, one of the greatest of Englishmen; after Shakespeare, Newton and Faraday perhaps the very greatest. When Johnson and the great actor David Garrick decided in 1737 to go to London to try their fortunes, they had only one horse between them. Undaunted, Johnson describes how they 'walked and tied,' setting off together, one riding horseback and the

Lichfield, in southern Staffordshire, is renowned for its three-towered Gothic cathedral, and also as the birthplace of Britain's famous lexicographer Dr Johnson and the home of the renowned actor/manager David Garrick. In 1737 they set out together to conquer London and when, after 30 years in the rough-and-tumble of the contemporary theatre, Garrick died, Johnson wrote: 'His death eclipsed the gaiety of nations and impoverished the harmless stock of human pleasure.' He had a magnificent funeral and his coffin was carried by several members of the nobility. His great strength and support throughout this career was his wife. After the funeral Mrs Garrick told her friend Hannah More that she went home, 'prayed with great composure, then kissed the dear bed and got into it with a sad pleasure'.

other walking. The horseman soon outstripped the walker, but then, after 5 to 6 miles (8–10 km), dismounted, tied the horse to a gate post and walked on. Soon the walker reached the tied horse, mounted it and rode on, passed his comrade after a further 6 or 7 miles (10–11 km) then tied the horse and did his stint of walking. So they shuttled to London using a single steed.

East of Birmingham, fondly known as 'Brummagem', is Coventry, source of the beautiful legend of Lady Godiva who, in order to save the lives of some

wrongly condemned citizens, volunteered to ride naked through the city to prove their innocence to her husband Count Leofric, and succeeded. As a prime industrial centre Coventy suffered some of the most savage air attacks of the Second World War, but rose to build itself into a fine modern city.

To the south-west is the county of Hereford and Worcester and to the south Warwickshire and Gloucestershire. Here is a cluster of lovely places. In Stratford-upon-Avon was born the world's finest poet, a country

The skeleton of the blitzed Coventry Cathedral seen through a window of the noble building which replaced it. As a prime industrial centre in the West Midlands, Coventry received more punishment in the Second World War than any other British city except perhaps London. But with the grit and dedication which characterized the heartland of industrial Britain, Coventry's citizens launched an ambitious rebuilding programme. The competition for designing the new cathedral was won by Sir Basil Spence who evolved the ingenious plan of building the new one in and around the ruins of the old.

lad of deep intelligence and wide grasp of human nature who, like Winston Churchill, failed to shine at his grammar school – which still stands – but who went to London and drank in all it had to offer of kingship and courtship, of soldiering and seamanship, of tavern and brothel, of love and hate, of all that the world's greatest city had in abundance; then cross-fertilized it with the fields and flowers, the jealousies and simplicities of his humble home town and the imperishable landscape in which it is set. Nearby is Charlecote and the woodlands in which he is supposed to have been caught poaching by its owner, Sir Thomas Lucy; Edge Hill and Worcester, the sites of two of the fiercest battles of the Civil War, waged 30-odd years after his death; and Broadway and Chipping

Camden, delightful examples of the honey-coloured villages, beautiful to the point of rapture, that adorn one of the finest areas of natural beauty England can boast, the Cotswold Hills and their surroundings.

To the south-west, on the broad Severn plain, is Cheltenham, a fine spa town to which generals and admirals retire in old age, as they do to Harrogate in North Yorkshire and Tunbridge Wells in Kent. Some people frown upon these handsome resting places, but what would its residents do in Butlin's Skegness Fun Palace, and what would lovers of Skegness do in Cheltenham? They represent wide extremes of taste and preference which are one of the hall-marks of a thriving democracy. I have a personal attachment to Cheltenham.

Nash's House, Stratford-upon-Avon, is a reminder that the Elizabethans were fond of formal gardens. We can imagine Sir Toby Belch, Maria and Feste in Twelfth Night *hiding behind a clipped yew hedge as Malvolio shows off his cross-gartered yellow stockings and reads aloud the love letter he believes to be from Olivia. The Elizabethans were also proud of their orchards. When, later in the play, Sir Toby urges Sir Andrew Aguecheek to summon up his courage and face Sebastian sword to sword, he says that Sebastian, 'bloody as the hunter, attends thee at the orchard-end'.*

All that we see of most castles is what has been left over after centuries of assault and battery; then we read the guide book, study the ground plan of the original stronghold and leave it at that. But Warwick Castle is complete: bastions, turrets, curtain walls, the lot – with the River Avon acting as part of its defensive moat. Moreover it has been in the family of the present Earl for the best part of four centuries. The name Warwick rings a bell in the minds even of schoolchildren, who immediately add to his name the title 'King-maker'. They could also add that the Earls of Warwick were among the foremost of those medieval barons whose power and greed bedevilled British national life for over 300 years, and whose internecine feuding was cut short only at Bosworth Field when Henry Tudor took a ruthless grip of the country's affairs.

Back in the 1870s, my mother, a young girl from Castle Douglas in Galloway, in south-western Scotland, got her first job as a housemaid with a Mrs Makepeace at a house on Leckhampton Hill near Cheltenham. I have a letter she sent home to her mother saying: 'Mrs Makepeace is very kind and says she is pleased with me and will I write you her compliments and she has raised my money to eight shillings a week. So I am very happy here.'

South-west of Cheltenham is Gloucester, a city founded by the Romans, with its magnificent cathedral and the famous *Lavatorium* where the monks washed each morning in cold water. (*Lavare* is the Latin word for *wash*. More intimate exercises were performed in the rere-dorter). There are also stairs deeply indented by millions of sandled foot-steps as the monks padded from their dormitory to a fresh round of praise and prayer in the choir below. Periodically the cathedral rings to the music of the famous Three Choirs Festival, one of the glories of British musical life, which Gloucester shares with the cathedrals in Hereford and Worcester. This festival, which began in 1724, has celebrated, especially in the last 50 years the name and fame of one of the most illustrious of British composers, Sir Edward Elgar.

142

Below: The River Avon runs through Stratford alongside Holy Trinity Church where Shakespeare was buried. Still to be seen are Shakespeare's birthplace and the grammar school where he learned 'small Latin and less Greek', but much about human behaviour and the surrounding countryside. When Shakespeare went to London the drama was already fully grown and waiting for him. He produced more than 30 plays between about 1591 and 1611, plus six long poems and 150 sonnets.

Bottom: The Beauchamp Chapel in the Church of St Mary's, hard by Warwick Castle, contains the tomb of Richard Beauchamp, Earl of Warwick, centre, and, left, a monument to Robert Dudley, Earl of Leicester and favourite of the Queen. Richard Beauchamp was the Earl of Warwick whom Bernard Shaw depicts in his St Joan, playing a prime role in Joan's capture, trial and eventual martyrdom in 1431.

143

Right: To the layman polo, as played here at Cirencester ('Cissester' to the locals), appears to be at least ten times as difficult as golf. The ball has to be hit by a surface only 3 inches (8 cm) in diameter and you have no time to judge the line or distance and no time to follow through. The co-operation of man with animal must be deeply satisfying.

Below: Arlington Row at Bibury, in the Cotswold Hills of Gloucestershire, is a string of tiny cottages, formerly a 14th-century wool store, but converted in the 17th century into a row of workmen's cottages. It is now one of the showpieces of old-time life in the county. I made my film Tawny Pipit in Little Slaughter, a short distance north of Bibury, and a few years later Chance of a Lifetime, written by myself and my old friend Walter Greenwood, author of Love on the Dole. The film was about the owner of a small factory who, sick of wild-cat strikes, lets the workers run the factory themselves.

Before entering Gloucester Cathedral, you must salute the memorial to its brave Bishop Hooper, a radical churchman who adopted Protestant views. One of the advance guard of church reformers, he served a spell in Fleet Prison for refusing to wear vestments and was sentenced for heresy and burned at the stake in 1555. Then pass through the arch and see the full glory of the cathedral, one of Britain's finest, especially famous for its deeply hollowed night stairs, down which monks padded to sing the Office, and the unique lavatorium (wash-room) with its vision of ice-cold ablutions in November! Such small domestic details give a truly vivid picture of monastic life and its discomforts. In the cathedral nave is the tomb of Edward II, murdered at nearby Berkeley Castle in 1327.

West of Gloucester, beyond the charming Forest of Dean, is Symond's Yat, a spectacular part of the Wye valley, set in a rural paradise. To the north are the Malvern Hills which William Langland, one of England's earliest poets and author of the *Vision of Piers Plowman* (c 1362), celebrated in his exquisite lines:

'Ac on a May morwenynge on Malverne hilles
Me bifel a ferly, of Fairye me thoghte.
I was wery forwandred and wente me to reste
Under a brood bank by a bourne syde.'

Malvern itself has a fine little theatre, where Bernard Shaw first launched many of his plays, and where many of Britain's finest actors and actresses found not only a cradle, but also a much prized shop window.

Left above: Symonds Yat on the River Wye, Gloucestershire, is one of the half dozen most celebrated beauty spots of Britain. Yat Rock was left behind as the Wye carved a deep valley between Ross and Chepstow. So here we have a glorious landscape laid out almost as if it were at our feet, a view from the gods of a river winding through the lush green of the valley. The river makes a great curve best seen from the Gloucestershire side. Who Symond was we have no record, but Yat is the same word as gaet or gate. All too often we read on gates the word 'Private' or 'No Thoroughfare' or 'Trespassers will be Prosecuted'. So Symond did us a good turn when he let us pass through this one.

Above: A field of mustard in Gloucestershire was probably planted in order to be ploughed in later as a fertilizer. English mustard is most commonly used with roast beef, but large emporia sell many variants, both black and white varieties mixed with a selection of delicate herbs in order to cool it. Mustard baths were once the common remedy for colds. Your mother stirred some into a bath of hot water and when you were immersed covered you and the bath with a large towel until you sweated. If the first dose failed, she added more boiling water and a second tablespoon of mustard. And we must never forget that the four fairies commanded by Titania to wait upon Bottom the Weaver in Shakespeare's A Midsummer Night's Dream were Peaseblossom, Cobweb, Moth and Mustardseed, which confirms mustard's ancient pedigree.

Below: Anne Hathaway's cottage at Shottery, close to Stratford and pleasantly removed from prying eyes, was surrounded by countryside ready to take a pair of young lovers to its heart. It was the home of a couple lower in the social scale than the Shakespeares, and a daughter ready to be seduced by the eldest son of a general merchant. After a few years of marriage the young husband decided to leave for London, sensing that he could write plays better than those he had recently seen, so the dye was cast. I see him as a lively, attractive lad as so many great artists have been.

Left: This apple orchard is in the Vale of Evesham, in the county of Hereford and Worcester, where some of Britain's finest fruit-growing country can be found. The Vale is also known for plums and I knew from the age of five that Pershore plums were the best you could buy. In 1265 Evesham was the site of the final battle between the forces of Henry III, whose parliament consisted largely of barons and prelates, and those of Simon de Montfort, who aimed to include representatives from the shires, towns and boroughs – a giant stride towards the democracy we enjoy today. Trapped by the King's army, de Montfort was overwhelmed and died surrounded by a few faithful followers. But the concept of broader parliamentary representation lived on, never to be reversed. Whenever you eat an apple or a plum remember Simon de Montfort.

Below: Shakespeare's birthplace in Stratford-upon-Avon is the home of a fairly comfortably off family. In contemporary records Shakespeare's father is spoken of as a glover, a dealer in wool and corn, and a butcher. All his trades were rooted in the real world and set in a lush countryside – the perfect grounding for a sensitive, intelligent lad with sharp eyes, a fine memory and a rich sense of humour invaluable for identifying such characters as Trinculo and Stephano, justices Shallow and Silence, Bottom the Weaver, Mistresses Page and Quickly and possibly a Doll Tearsheet or two, broken-down servicemen like Pistol and Bardolph and Falstaff himself, with of course a wealth of blushing rural Juliets. Add the world of courtship and majesty to this repertoire and the budding dramatist is on his way. The idea that Shakespeare was really the Earl of Southampton or Francis Bacon is one that the British have rightly refused to embrace.

Ludlow, to the north in Shropshire, contains the remains of a Norman castle planted there, as were so many others, to hold back the wild and unruly Welsh who cared not a fig for Romans, Saxons, Vikings, Norsemen, nor indeed for anyone else. When my wife and I were staying with friends in Anglesey, I ventured to ask a labourer in a local pub how he felt about the English and other intruders. He replied seriously but without venom: 'If we had our way we would build a high wall right the way round Wales so that nobody could get in and no-one could get out that is how we feel about you cheerio.'

Shropshire is the 'coloured' county of A E

Above: The Manor House at Lower Brockhampton, Hereford and Worcester, was already 200 years old when Shakespeare was born. The buildings hark back to more dangerous times when the countryside harboured cutpurses and vagabonds, and if you lived in a substantial home out in the country you took the precaution of digging a moat and planting a strong gatehouse to guard it. 'Hark, hark, the dogs do bark, The beggars are coming to town!' – better safe than sorry.

Housman's *A Shropshire Lad*, one of the books which, along with those of Thomas Hardy and Gerard Manley Hopkins, helped English poetry to break the deadlock of Victorian and Edwardian models and find a new and modern voice. One poem, 'Bredon Hill', begins:

'In summertime on Bredon
    The bells they sound so clear;
Round both the shires they ring them
    In steeples far and near,
    A happy noise to hear.

Here of a Sunday morning
    My love and I would lie,
And see the coloured counties,
    And hear the larks so high
    About us in the sky.'

To the north Coalbrookdale, in the shadow of the Wrekin, that strange remnant of an ancient volcano, was the home of Abraham Darby, who realized that timber structuring had to give way to metal. He set his seal on the new age by building the first iron bridge in 1779. This beautiful structure spans the River Severn in the Ironbridge Gorge, near Coalbrookdale. At a single stroke, Darby ushered in the fire, smoke and fury which we call the Industrial Revolution and which gave Britain a long lead in the race for world ascendancy throughout the 19th century and well into the 20th.

In this unforgettable stretch of England, we must not neglect Shrewsbury, because it was only a short distance to the north of the town that in 1403 the battle took place in which King Henry IV and his brilliant son met the greatest challenge of his career, the revolt of the Northumbrians led by Henry Percy, 'the Hotspur of the North' and the fabled Welsh warrior Owen Glendower. Many people opt for *Hamlet* as Shakespeare's greatest play, but for a vision of medieval England, there is nothing to compare with the histories, notably the two parts of *Henry IV* and *Henry V*, with their picture of heroism and treachery, of riotous tavern life in London and domestic felicities in faraway Gloucestershire. And Shakespeare's final injunction in *The Life and Death of King John* is as true today as it ever was:

'Nought shall make us rue,
If England to itself do rest but true.'

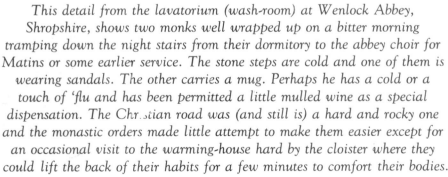

This detail from the lavatorium (wash-room) at Wenlock Abbey, Shropshire, shows two monks well wrapped up on a bitter morning tramping down the night stairs from their dormitory to the abbey choir for Matins or some earlier service. The stone steps are cold and one of them is wearing sandals. The other carries a mug. Perhaps he has a cold or a touch of 'flu and has been permitted a little mulled wine as a special dispensation. The Christian road was (and still is) a hard and rocky one and the monastic orders made little attempt to make them easier except for an occasional visit to the warming-house hard by the cloister where they could lift the back of their habits for a few minutes to comfort their bodies.

Ironbridge, Shropshire, supports the strange fact that engineers often come up with more beautiful objects than architects. Brunel's suspension bridge at Clifton, Bristol, Telford's Menai bridge, the new bridges over the Severn and Firth of Forth, and scores of modern bridges over motorways, are good examples. And, in the vanguard, Abraham Darby's iron bridge, spanning the Severn near Coalbrookdale in Shropshire, which is more than 200 years old. The first fumblings towards the use of a new material are often clumsy, but here Darby made a great leap forward, realizing that iron could be bent into circles and ellipses in a way that timber and stone never could be. A masterpiece!

153

Higher Town Bay is on St Martin's in the Scilly Isles. Although you hear the names of only a few of them – St Mary's, St Martin's, Tresco, St Agnes and Bryher – the Scilly Isles number about 150, lying some 27 miles (43 km) west of Land's End in Cornwall. They are remnants of a huge mass of granite formed around 300 million years ago. Legend says that they are the remains of the drowned kingdom of Atlantis, which was supposed to have been in the Atlantic Ocean according to Plato (c 427–347 BC). The legend probably came into being more than 3,400 years ago, when a volcano on the Greek island of Thera (or Santorini) erupted, causing huge waves which contributed to the destruction of the Minoan civilization of Crete. What a wonderful addition to Britain's island history it would be if the Scilly Isles were ever found to be part of the vanished Atlantis.

The South and South-West

Sailing in from the south-west, a passenger's first glimpse of England is the Scillies, that group of small, low islands which, warmed by the Gulf Stream, produce the country's earliest spring flowers – daffodils, bluebells, narcissi and crocuses. A little farther east are the gaunt granite cliffs of Land's End and the mystical land of Cornwall, inhabited by the Celts who are also Methodists, a mellow and formidable mixture. Here are occasionally seen women of typical Celtic beauty, with sea-grey eyes and raven-black hair. The ancient Celtic language died out in the early years of the present century, although Cornish nationalists have recently been reviving it. But the last person to speak Cornish and no other language was Dolly Pentreath, who was my secretary's great-great grandmother. She died in 1777.

The Celts came to England about 2,500 years ago, but evidence of earlier Stone and Bronze Age peoples is scattered over southern and south-western England in the form of standing stones, ruined villages, and such vast cathedral-sized structures as Wiltshire's Stonehenge and Avebury. There are also figures carved in the hillsides, such as the giant of Cerne Abbas, a naked man 180 feet (55 metres) high, brandishing a club which is 121 feet (37 metres) long. We can only guess at the meaning of these monuments and hill figures. Some were probably concerned with the movements of the stars and the changing seasons, some with the deeper mysteries of life, death and the hereafter, and some, like the Cerne Abbas giant, with questions of fertility.

If the Sun and Moon failed to rise, or if people failed to produce children, mankind would be doomed. In Victorian times such things were not discussed. Nevertheless, until quite recently, couples still went out on moonlit nights and slept together between the thighs of the Cerne Abbas giant. The gods of Earth and Heaven

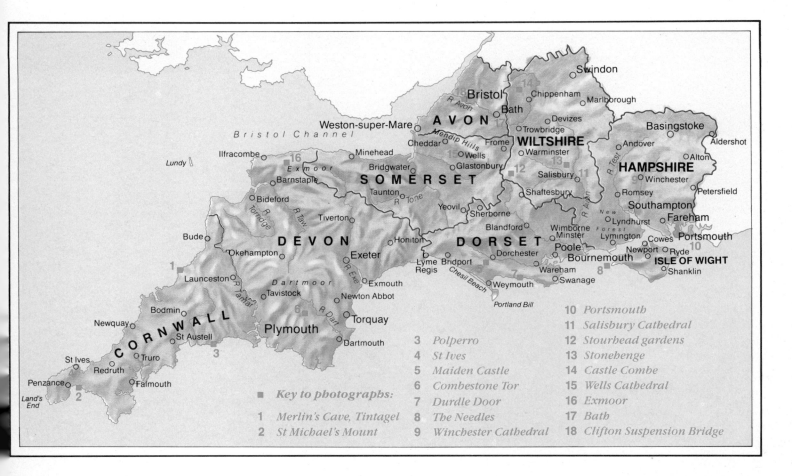

Key to photographs:
1 Merlin's Cave, Tintagel
2 St Michael's Mount
3 Polperro
4 St Ives
5 Maiden Castle
6 Combestone Tor
7 Durdle Door
8 The Needles
9 Winchester Cathedral
10 Portsmouth
11 Salisbury Cathedral
12 Stourhead gardens
13 Stonehenge
14 Castle Combe
15 Wells Cathedral
16 Exmoor
17 Bath
18 Clifton Suspension Bridge

Merlin's Cave is at Tintagel, Cornwall. At the Battle of Hastings in 1066, Britain was conquered and brute force had won the day. Something gentle was needed to restore the pride of the defeated English, and what better than to flatter them by telling them of a great king named Arthur who, with his followers, had done wonderful deeds. In the 12th century, a Welsh monk, Geoffrey of Monmouth, wrote the story down and got minstrels to sing it. The story told how a wizard, Merlin, arranged for the birth of a special baby who grew up to be King Arthur, and how King Arthur gathered brave men around him at Camelot and how they had many adventures. Tintagel, where there was a fine castle, was chosen as Arthur's birthplace, and Geoffrey of Monmouth told how Merlin lived in a cave beneath the castle. If you want to read the story of Arthur, I recommend Tales of King Arthur *by James Riordan and illustrated by Victor Ambrus.*

supposedly whispered to the couples, who were then assured of producing fine children. It is rumoured that elderly businessmen from the City of London, seeking some measure of rejuvenation, have followed the same procedure and have been rewarded by their favourite secretaries on top of well-padded office desks.

When the Romans came down to the West Country, the Britons fought fiercely for their homeland behind skilfully built fortifications. The finest of these is Maiden Castle near Dorchester. This magnificent hill-top encampment girdled by ramparts and a ditch, had a cleverly designed double entrance to fool and entrap unwary invaders. It took the Romans a mighty effort to subdue Maiden Castle. Witness an iron bolt buried in the spine of one defender and found by archaeologists – a vivid and moving testimony of a life and death struggle.

These western lands are also full of myth and legend. One of the first tales I ever heard was 'Jack the Giant Killer'. Jack's boast was clear and strong:

'I am Jack the Cornishman,
Who slew the giant Cormoran.'

The greatest of all British legends, that of King Arthur and his Knights of the Round Table, is also rooted in the West Country. In the fourth and fifth centuries AD, when the Roman Empire was under attack by Barbarians from Asia, its soldiers were called home, leaving Britain open to attacks by the Saxons from Denmark and Holland.

157

St Michael's Mount is a granite island dominating Mount's Bay. It is surmounted by a magnificent castle – a romantic vision indeed. At low tide you can walk across to it along a causeway. In the 1940s I acted here with Michael Wilding and Sally Gray in the film of Compton Mackenzie's Carnival, staying with a lovely lady named Mrs Matthews whose late husband had been a Cornish tin miner. She told me that the old miners were deeply Christian and she gave me a small rectangular tray made of pure tin and stamped 'Chyandour', the name of the mine where it had been produced. It also carried a picture of a lamb (the Lamb of God), holding a flag with a cross on it. Tin mining was dangerous; it was as well to keep on the safe side of evil in case of accidents. I still have the tray at my bedside.

158

But in the West Country a great leader arose who repelled the invaders in a number of fierce battles. His name was Artorius or Arcturius, Latin words for Arthur. Arthur's name and fame lived on after his death, and accounts of his life were embellished by minstrels and story-tellers, who added fresh characters and adventures. Gradually, the story of Arthur changed from history into what we call myth which is history raised to a higher level. In this case, the story-tellers combined the Arthurian legend with another, telling how, after Jesus was crucified, his friend and disciple, Joseph of Arimathea brought to England a piece of the Cross on which our Lord had suffered, also the Golden Chalice which He and His disciples used at the Last Supper. The Holy Spirit led Joseph to Glastonbury in northern Somerset, and there he planted the fragment of the Cross which took root. It

Polperro, one of Cornwall's most popular and attractive holiday resorts, is full of colour-washed cottages leading down steep, narrow lanes to a tiny harbour. Apart from tourism, it earns its living from pilchard fishing, using a net called a seine which has floats on top and weights beneath, so encircling the fish like a hanging curtain. Cornwall is strongly individual, with a rich dialect incomprehensible to Cockneys, Geordies, Black Country folk, Scots and Welsh, just as their own speech is largely incomprehensible to the Cornish. Cornish folk believe in the 'wee people', whom the English call elves, the Irish leprechauns, but which they call pixies. They well know that you must take every precaution against your babies being bewitched, or 'pixilated', by these mischievous little creatures.

Top: Combestone Tor is an impressive granite outcrop about 10 miles (16 km) east of Tavistock. It looks man-made, almost like a piece of modern sculpture. The granite was formed millions of years ago from molten material far below the surface, and as it solidified it became jointed. Weathering has gradually eaten away along the joints. Not far from Combestone Tor are two impressive 'clapper' bridges made of granite slabs cunningly supported on uprights sunk into the river bed. Dartmoor is rich in evidence of early habitation in the form of standing stones and other monuments going back 4,000 or 5,000 years and possibly more.

Above: Fisherman survey their catch at St Ives. Cornwall's waters are famous for pilchards, but these look to me more like salmon bass. Cornwall has hazardous coasts and the iron in them pulled compasses out of true, bringing many a ship to grief. Some claim that the locals used to set signal lamps in the wrong places in order to make sure of a good wreck. It is said that a Cornish prayer runs as follows: 'Oh Lord, if this night it be Thy intention, to raise a storm and wreck a ship, we beseech Thee let it be wrecked as near as possible to Polperro, so that Thy loving servants in this parish may have the benefit of any useful articles that may happen to be washed ashore.'

Top: When I was a small boy we had sing-songs around the piano with my Uncle Ernie rendering his favourite number. He had a deep bass voice and always sang flat out, really loud, a song that started by telling us that Devon had rich red loam and finished with the chorus:

> 'Old England's counties by the sea
> From east to west be seven,
> But the gem of that fair galaxy
> Is Devon, Glorious Devon!'

This photograph of Devonian farmland might have been taken specially for him.

Above: Maiden Castle is Britain's greatest testimony to the success of the Stone Age and the greatest monument to its people. The biggest early hilltop fortress in Europe, it was first occupied in about 2000 BC. It met its greatest challenge in AD 43 when it was assaulted by the Romans and, after a long and hard-fought struggle, was taken. Excavations have unearthed much evidence of the fanatical resistance put up by its defenders against the highly professional and superbly organized Roman legions.

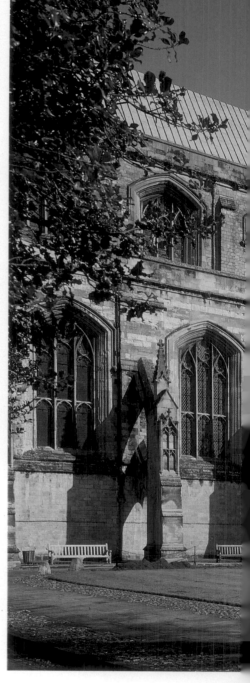

was here that the first English abbey was built, high up on Glastonbury Tor. Somehow the two legends were spliced together. The Saxons were heathen, Arthur was a Christian. Hence Arthur's knights went out to fight evil. If they fought it bravely and successfully, they would see the precious Holy Grail, which was supposed to be kept in a mysterious building called 'The Chapel Perilous' in the middle of a dark wood.

Visitors to Glastonbury find this story flooding over them and many come to believe it. Glastonbury is associated in the Arthurian legend with the Vale of Avalon, which contained the lake from which the hand was raised to receive back Arthur's sacred sword, and where the black funeral barge bore away his dead body. Somerset contains some of Europe's most beautiful countryside, including the limestone Mendip Hills in the north, with their spectacular Cheddar Gorge, the Quantock Hills, and the lion's share of the breathtaking Exmoor National Park which spills over into Devon.

The coasts of Avon, Somerset, Devon, Cornwall, Dorset, Hampshire and the Isle of Wight contain many beautiful resorts and delightful fishing villages, such as Mullion Cove in Cornwall where I spent six happy weeks filming *Never Let Me Go* with Clark Gable and Gene

Previous spread: Tides and currents have battered away at both sides of a limestone headland and finally broken through to form Durdle Door. Durdle Door is near Lulworth Cove, one of Dorset's best-loved beauty spots, and Weymouth, my favourite seaside resort, if only because it has not been modernized. Our family took summer holidays at Weymouth for many years before the First World War, largely because my father trusted only the Great Western Railway and would travel by no other. At Frome we lined up in the corridor to see the White Horse cut in the Wiltshire hillside. Then on to Weymouth, which has the longest and safest sands in Britain.

Above left: A lighthouse warns ships of the Needles and the Isle of Wight. Sailing in from the west at night or in overcast weather, you could easily be wrecked on the western end of the island, for the passage to Southampton past Alum, Totland and Colwell Bays is narrow and irregular and requires expert navigation. Heaven knows how many ships lie on the seabed around the Needles, lost in storm, fog or pitch darkness before the lighthouse was built. The lighthouse is planted on the western end of a chalk ridge which runs right through the island, striking out in the west in these sharp, chalk stacks. The chalk used in classrooms is fragile, being made of the soft mineral gypsum. But the rock chalk, a type of limestone, possesses great power to resist erosion as the Needles testify.

Above: Winchester Cathedral, one of Britain's holy places was built upon ground already sacred as the capital city of Britain's greatest monarch, Alfred the Great. Inside these walls breathes his giant spirit. Warrior, saint and visionary, he inspired resistance to the heathen Danes and kept the Christian flag flying in the western part of the country, laying the foundations of a civilized Britain, including a vision of the Royal Navy. The cathedral, founded in 1079 and consecrated in 1093, was added to over the succeeding centuries. The bodies of many early Danish kings, including Canute, lie inurned in caskets high up on shelves in the Cathedral's noble choir. Years ago, when she was only seven, I took my daughter Sally into the cathedral and when she saw these caskets and I explained that the kings inside them were waiting for Resurrection, she said: 'Like the left luggage department at Waterloo Station?' 'Something like that', I replied.

Right: Apart from those used by the police, cavalry units and brewers, there are not too many working horses about these days, so ploughing matches, like this one in Hampshire, are a rarity, whereas up to the 1940s they were the crowning events of village fairs all over Britain. Horse ploughing was recognized as a truly great skill requiring a perfect admixture of eye and hand. Here the Shire horses have cut a furrow and the ploughman is cleaning some clay from the share or mould-board before going round the headland to cut one in the opposite direction. If he had a 'turn-wrest' or one-way plough, he would merely spin the coulter and mould-board around and return the way he came, only throwing the furrow the opposite way.

166

Left: Portsmouth is a seaport and naval base inseparably linked with HMS Victory, Nelson's flagship at the Battle of Trafalgar. News of the battle and of Nelson's death arrived in London many days after the event and then by strange means. Brick towers had been built at intervals most of the way from Portsmouth to the Admiralty in Whitehall, London – at Southsea, Bedhampton, Petersfield, Harting, Midhurst, Haslemere, Witley, Guildford, Cobham, Esher, Kingston, Putney and Chelsea – each carrying on its roof a stout post with long hinged arms, called a semaphore, and the signal was passed from hill to hill, reaching the Admiralty in a few minutes.

Above: Salisbury Cathedral, built between 1220 and 1280, is one of the jewels of British architecture, largely because it was planned (by Bishop Richard Poore) and completed (by his young brother) within 60 years, while most British cathedrals grew up over the centuries. That is part of their fascination, for they tell a country's history in terms of stone, timber and workmen who could not remember when the building of their cathedral had begun. But many a boy born around 1207 in Salisbury, who helped to dig the Cathedral's foundations, must have lived to join in the celebrations at its completion. My sculptor son-in-law Roy Noakes helped to carve the huge stone eagle at the corner of Barclays Bank Head Office, in London's Lombard Street, and whenever we drove past it my granddaughter would say in a very loud voice: 'My daddy made that', recalling tiny tots in Salisbury who boasted about what their forefathers had done 700 years earlier.

167

Tierney way back in 1954. There is also some of Europe's finest cliff scenery, winding estuaries, secluded bays and coves, and many striking features, such as Chesil Beach, a wave-tossed bank of shingle linking mainland Dorset to the former Isle of Portland, and also the dazzling chalk stacks, called The Needles, off the western tip of the Isle of Wight. Most of these magnificent coastlands are now protected as Areas of Outstanding Natural Beauty.

Around Cornwall's rugged coasts, the seabed is littered with wrecks. This is partly because the rocks contain iron, which plays havoc with ships' compasses. Losing their way and caught in the wrong wind, many ships have been dragged remorselessly towards the shore. In the first scene of Shakespeare's *The Tempest*, a ship's company tries to stop their vessel running aground. The former Poet Laureate John Masefield, who served in

Stourhead, Wiltshire, is famous for one of the most beautiful landscape gardens in Britain, laid out by Henry Hoare, son of a banker, around 1741. The days of formal Elizabethan and Jacobean gardens were over, and freer, more informal patterns were taking their place. Here we have a cunningly designed garden which looks perfectly natural, as if that was how it had sprung up, with lakes and a tiny Greek temple, conifers, beeches, rhododendrons, tulip-trees and many other rare plants and shrubs. It forms a worthy setting for the stately home itself, a Palladian mansion brimming over with art treasures.

Good straw thatch will last for 40 or 50 years and reed thatch twice as long. Like every other craftsman, the thatcher, here at work rethatching a cottage in Somerset, has his own special tools, including a leggatt, a biddle, a drift, a yoke, an eave-hook and a shearing hook. As robots take over more and more of our handwork, I believe that opportunities for people to take up the fascinating and deeply satisfying crafts that can be performed by the most beautiful of all instruments – the human hand – will increase. And thatching stands high among those crafts.

square-riggers as a boy, told me that this scene gives a perfect picture of a sailing ship bearing down on what is known as 'a lee shore'. Perhaps Shakespeare who, as far as we know, never went to sea, got the details of the scene from old shellbacks like Francis Drake or Walter Raleigh.

Drake, Raleigh, Richard Grenville, John Hawkins and other great mariners of the 16th century were all Devonians. They secured for themselves a special place in the affections of Good Queen Bess, by guaranteeing the country's security and bringing back loot from the Spanish Main. Unintimidated by fancy court speech, they also injected some rich West Country accents into the speech of London society. The home of Francis Drake, at Buckland Abbey, south of Tavistock, is now a museum, with such relics as Drake's sword and drum.

Left: Castle Combe in north-western Wiltshire. The English village is, at its best, one of the loveliest of inventions. A church, often built among ancient yew trees, the manor house, the vicarage, the school, the carpenter's shop, the stone-mason's, the blacksmith's, the grocer's, the thatcher's and the general store, rounded off by a public house or two and a cluster of dwelling houses – the whole thing set among lanes and farms: a community, an entity. Weddings, Easter, Christmas and Armistice Day all fitted together like a well-made table; hard work, good food, economy, charity, tolerance and the certainty of a reward in Heaven.

Below: An overpowering sense of purpose and achievement meets visitors to Stonehenge, seen here at dawn. Forty years ago archaeologists dated it as belonging to 1200 BC. Now carbon dating techniques have pushed that figure back a further 2,000 years and maybe beyond, just like the dating of the emergence of Mankind, which in the 1930s was thought to be around 30,000 years ago. Now the figure is more like two million.

Above: Wells Cathedral is mercifully set in a huge village green so that you can get far enough away to see it properly, especially its glorious west front, decorated with more than 300 figures of prophets, patriarchs, saints and angels, all queuing up for opening time in Paradise. 'Move along there, and no pushing!' I believe that the British habit of forming orderly queues was early rooted and that this is a representation of the fact. Do not miss the cathedral's superb north porch, its glorious Lady Chapel, or the Bishop's Palace guarded by its own moat. The museum planted on the north-eastern corner of the cathedral was largely arranged by my old friend Norman Cook, one of the founding fathers of the London Museum and a star performer in the television programme 'Animal, Vegetable and Mineral' some years ago.

It is not just the coasts of the West Country that are beautiful. Inland lie Bodmin Moor in Cornwall and the majestic Dartmoor National Park in Devon with its brooding granite tors and traces of prehistoric settlement; also ancient tin mines and charming villages, with houses built of wattle and daub, a mixture of clay and chalk puddled with cow dung; superb churches and fine cathedrals. Of these, three of the greatest are at Salisbury in Wiltshire, Wells in Somerset, and Winchester in Hampshire. Salisbury is the only English cathedral built within a fairly brief time span, thus displaying a single, uniform style. Wells is a masterpiece of medieval stonework, its west front composed almost entirely of patriarchs and saints standing before the gates of Paradise waiting their turn to be called in, while the cathedral at Winchester, once capital of Wessex, contains the bodies of early Saxon kings and queens, including old friends of our schooldays, Ethelred the Unready and Canute.

The West Country also contains dramatic evidence that Britain is not just a rural country living on its past. For example, the metal used in Brunel's exquisite Clifton suspension bridge in Bristol and other bridges too was forged in unlovely industrial cities. And Plymouth and

171

Portsmouth are bases for the steel ships built in Scotland and Northern Ireland amid the uproar of hammers and welding equipment by men equal in skill and sense of national purpose to their timber-working forefathers.

The men who build our cars are no less able and skilful than the men who built the cathedrals. The Austin 7, the Alvis, the Aston Martin, the Bentley, the Rolls-Royce and their forebears, many of which can be seen in my old friend Edward Montagu's magnificent museum at Beaulieu, are legitimate parts of 'Beautiful Britain', as are the giant railway engines built at Swindon, in northern Wiltshire, including *Mallard*, holder of the world's steam locomotive speed record and now retired to the Railway Museum at York; also the aircraft, from *Gypsy Moth* and *Percival Gull* to the Spitfires and Hurricanes of World War II, and the supersonic *Concorde*. All have a place in Britain's heritage. For Britain is not only a land of beauty spots, but also a great industrial country, full of people who can do anything with metal amid the smoke and flame of the Black Country and other centres of British industry. The inventors and craftsmen of the Industrial Revolution cry out to be remembered and celebrated.

The Black Mountains in Gwent form part of the Brecon Beacons National Park which runs in a wide 60-mile (97 km) curve from south-eastern Dyfed in the west through southern Powys into northern Gwent as if girdling the southern industrial lands and protecting the rest of Wales from their intrusion. South of Brecon is the highest peak in the Brecon Beacons, Pen y Fan, which is 2,907 feet (886 metres) high. It was used for centuries as a beacon. From its peak a light could signal north for reinforcements, westwards to warn of attack by the English, or eastwards to warn of an onslaught by Irish pirates of the kind who captured young St Patrick and thereby unwittingly converted Ireland to Christianity. Beacon signals were given by means of a 'cresset', a kind of metal canister filled with oil and mounted on a pole.

South Wales

Wales is one of the most beautiful lands on Earth, made up almost entirely of mountains and valleys and peopled by a race both friendly and uniquely communicative, also fiercely independent and individual, cherishing what is to foreigners a largely unpronounceable language, spoken with the world's most beautiful vowel sounds. Within its boundaries are the ruins of more than a hundred castles, built to keep the Welsh out of England and to help the English capture and hold on to as much as possible of Wales. Long ago the border between England and Wales was rarely secure. Battle swayed to and fro within a wide and ever-fluctuating arc called the Marches.

One of Wales's castles is at Monmouth on the River Wye, which forms part of the border between England and the Welsh county of Gwent. Here in 1387 a boy was born who, as Henry V, was destined to divert the nation's attention from his father's tenuous claims to the throne by a series of brilliant but quite unnecessary military exploits overseas. South of Monmouth, in a bend of the Wye, are the lovely ruins of the 12th-century Tintern Abbey, associated for ever with William Wordsworth's 'Lines, composed a few miles above Tintern Abbey' (1798), which celebrates nature as:

> 'A motion and a spirit, that impels
> All thinking things, all objects of all thought,
> And rolls through all things.'

Also in Gwent is Caerleon, near Newport, where the Romans planted a powerful fortress and manned it with two of their finest legions. Parts of it, including the amphitheatre, can still be seen.

In neighbouring Mid Glamorgan is Caerphilly with its mighty castle, which is second in size only to Windsor,

The original Cardiff Castle was little more than a Roman fortress, but the Normans transformed it into a true stronghold which has been enlarged and developed over the years. Cardiff is a great seaport where you can see and feel the energy, the ingenuity, the basic strength and purpose of the Welsh people in wrestling with their precious soil and glorious landscape, persuading it to give them a living. Cardiff is known the world over as the headquarters of rugby football. That and the gift of song bring together the body and soul of a unique people. Had coal and iron not been discovered in its southern valleys in the mid-19th century Wales would have remained the paradise we see when we visit its protected regions.

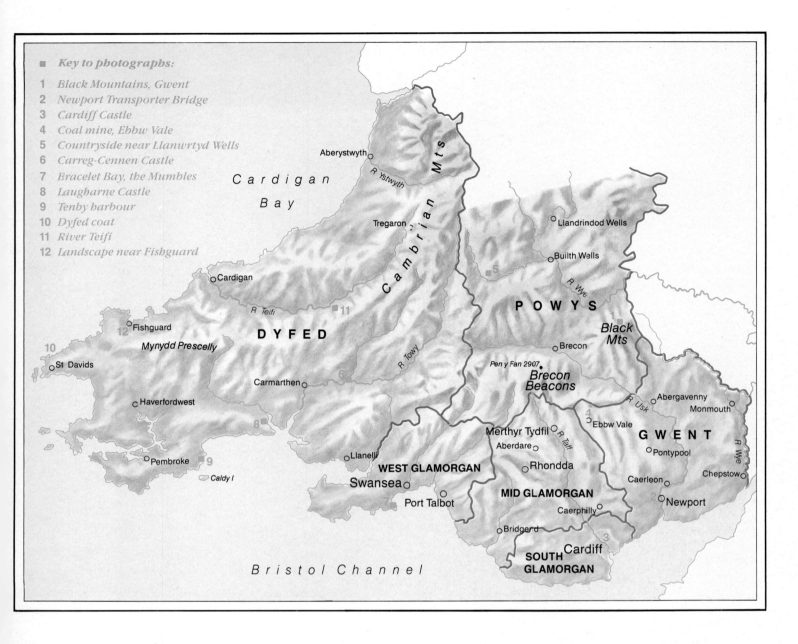

Left: Newport Transporter Bridge is an unusual and highly original structure, best described as a sort of mid-air ferry carrying people and cars across the estuary of the River Usk by means of a cable-car 250 feet (76 metres) above the water. Nearby Caerleon is famous as the easternmost strong-point of the Roman army, a huge encampment able to hold a couple of legions each 1,500 strong. With Caerleon to secure the southern corner of Wales and Chester the northern, the Romans could begin a wide encircling movement, advancing westwards on two wings, forcing the centre to retreat in order to avoid being cut off altogether. The Romans built a civilian town a few miles to the rear of Caerleon to show that they were not casual visitors but potential residents.

while just north of Cardiff in South Glamorgan is Llandaff Cathedral, where Jacob Epstein's disturbing but, in the end, comforting statue of Christ in Majesty jolts visitors into a fresh vision of Christianity. Here is the place to offer a prayer (and drop a coin or two for the upkeep of the cathedral).

West of Cardiff, which is as busy and imposing as a capital city should be, is Saint Fagan's Folk Museum, housing domestic arts and crafts which have persisted over many centuries. Here that persistence is shown in terms of everyday life on field and farm – the early tools and techniques by which timber, iron and stone were put to the high purpose of fighting nature and then living hand in hand with her in creative collaboration. And at the Folk Museum traditional craftsmen demonstrate some of the techniques which brought that collaboration to perfection.

As if the taming of mountain and valley were not enough, the war with nature extended underground because here, in the 18th century, in the hills and valleys

of Glamorgan were found in vast quantities and of the highest quality the two indispensable handmaidens of the Industrial Revolution – coal and iron. The Welsh people took on this mighty and all-devouring challenge with a majestic courage and capacity for self-sacrifice unmatched in British history, except perhaps in Glasgow.

To the north, in the county of Powys, as if trying to restrain the incessant pressure of coal and steel, lies the Brecon Beacons National Park, watered by the River Usk and dominated by Pen y Fan, which rises to 2,907 feet (886 metres) and can, therefore, claim to be almost a genuine mountain. Not to be missed in the far west of the National Park is Carrig-Cennen Castle, a 14th-century fortress planted on a spectacular site.

One of our greatest gifts is our will to hold the balance between destruction and preservation. Population pressure and the need to increase production threaten the wild, the rare, the remote and the beautiful, so the will to destroy and the will to preserve are in constant collision. It has been necessary to make laws to protect ourselves against ourselves. The deep-seated will to preserve came to fruition with the establishment of National Parks and Areas of Outstanding Natural Beauty, which preserve as much as possible of our national heritage for all time.

One of the loveliest of these protected areas is the Gower Peninsula in West Glamorgan with its famous Mumbles Head immortalized a hundred years ago by the two brave daughters of its lighthouse-keeper, who saw a single survivor marooned on a shipwreck. When no one dared to brave the foaming breakers, they plunged in and

Above: In a land rich with castles built to shield their inhabitants from invaders and from each other, the 14th-century Carreg-Cennen in south-eastern Dyfed is one of the most dramatic. Built on the edge of a 300-foot (91-metre) high cliff, it is quite inaccessible and unassailable on that side. About 5 or 6 miles (8–10 km) to the west is Dryslwyn Castle, while a few miles to the north in the Vale of Twyi is Carn Goch, a huge Iron Age hill fortress comparable in scale with Maiden Castle in Dorset. England had its destructive tribalism knocked out of it at the Battle of Hastings, but it took much longer for the Welsh and Scots to lose theirs. Today it is expressed in rugby and cricket and in the crowds that support and sing for them.

Left: Bracelet Bay, at The Mumbles, is about 3 miles (5 km) south of Swansea, Wales's second largest city. This is the south-eastern tip of the Gower Peninsula, a popular tourist area with lovely beaches, a fine, cliff-lined coast and some of Wales's finest unspoiled scenery inland. Limestone caves in Gower are known to have been the homes of Stone Age fisher folk, who used hooks made of bones and lines of tough stems woven together. Wales is rich in relics of prehistoric Man – tumuli, cairns, dolmens, standing stones and Iron Age fortifications.

Above: The ancient and delightful old town of Laugharne can truly boast of its history, its 12th-century Charter kept in its tiny Town Hall, and the vestiges of medieval titles and procedures whereby it is still governed. But Laugharne is also where Dylan Thomas lived and wrote much of his finest poetry, in a humble boat-house just behind the castle. Here he was at home, his soul fed and blossomed, and his pen wove those unique passages which we now treasure. Here was a rich, rare and original voice of Wales.

Above: Tenby is on the southern side of the rocky Pembrokeshire promontory in southern Dyfed, perched on a headland overlooking Caldy Island to the south. This delightful little town is protected by 13th-century walls and looks down on a splendid harbour. Caldy Island boasts an old priory church and a modern monastery. From earliest times monks have tended to build their habitations as far away as possible from the hurly-burly of daily life, in places where they could sing, pray and praise God without interruption. Such a place is Caldy, isolated and yet still in touch with the world's affairs. Many of the names in south-western Dyfed have an English flavour – Bosherston, Pembroke, Milford, Angle, Haverford and so on. This is because the Normans encouraged English settlers to come and live here around 600 to 700 years ago.

Above right: Of Britain's ten National Parks, Wales has three of the most magnificent – Snowdonia, Brecon and, greatest of all, the Pembrokeshire Coast one. I say this because I love the sea and the rocky fastness between Laugharne and Cardigan is unsurpassed, providing a vision of human stature in the face of nature and of the long and unceasing battle we all wage between life and death. My own favourite words in the English language, words I try to live by, are in one of the sermons of John Donne: 'For this life is a business, and a perplexed business, a warfare and a bloody warfare, a voyage and a tempestuous voyage.' And I know no scene in nature that expresses this heroic challenge more completely than the Dyfed coast.

brought him safely ashore, winning for themselves, in Clement Scott's verses, a firm place in Britain's nautical poetry:

'Off went the women's shawls, sir; in a second
  they're torn and rent,
And knotting them into a rope of love, straight into
  the sea they went!
"Come back," cried the lighthouse-keeper, "for
  God's sake, girls, come back!"
As they caught the waves on their foreheads,
  resisting the fierce attack.
"Come back!" said the girls, "we will not! go tell it
  to all the town,
We'll lose our lives, God willing, before that man
  shall drown!
Give one more knot to your shawls, Bess! give one
  strong clutch of your hand!
Just follow me, brave, to the shingle, and we'll bring
  him safe to land!
Wait for the next wave, darling, only a minute more,
And I'll have him safe in my arms, dear, and we'll
  drag him safe to shore."
Up to their necks in the water, fighting it breast to
  breast,
They caught and saved a brother alive! God bless us,
  you know the rest.
Well, many a heart beat stronger, and many a tear
  was shed,
And many a glass was toss'd right off to "The
  Women of Mumbles Head!"'

183

Fishguard stands at the head of its own little harbour on the north side of Dyfed's ragged, storm-beaten promontory. An inscribed stone records how in 1797 a detachment of French infantry, part of an invasion force, was driven ashore at Fishguard only to be captured by a troop of local women dressed in traditional red· cloaks and thus mistaken for British Redcoats. More recently, a couple of a dozen of us spent a hazardous, character-forming two months here filming John Huston's Moby Dick, rowing back and forth in beautiful whale-boats made by a couple of old craftsmen in Whitby, North Yorkshire, who still remembered how they were fashioned.

A little farther west, in the county of Dyfed, is Laugharne which stands on the River Taf estuary. This was once the home of one of the most famous of all 20th-century Welshmen, Dylan Thomas. At Laugharne, in a tiny fisherman's hut, Thomas wrote much of his loveliest poetry and many of his finest letters, wrestling words into quite fresh and unexpected associations, reaching new and heart-breaking levels of beauty. West again there begins one of the longest stretches of protected coastline in Britain, including Tenby in the south-east, St Bride's Bay, St David's Head, Fishguard and beyond. Also protected are the islands of Skokholm and Skomer, which were 'adopted' by the famous naturalist R M Lockley back in the 1920s and turned into bird sanctuaries. He lived there for many years, alone in a small, derelict farmhouse, studying bird behaviour and their nesting and breeding habits, recording at first hand everything he saw and publishing it in the ornithological press, and in journals like the 'Countryman'.

St David's Head was the birthplace of Wales's patron saint, the sixth-century David (or Dewi). His tiny

cathedral stands on the site of a monastic settlement founded by himself. North-east of St David's Head is Fishguard, where I lived for two or three months during the filming of *Moby Dick*, Herman Melville's masterpiece. There we braved the angry waters of the Irish Sea much like the women of Mumbles Head, except that, in order to satisfy director John Huston's passion for verisimilitude, we were in whale-boats pulled at high speed by Royal Navy torpedo boats from Pembroke Dock and wearing two life-belts apiece in case of mishaps. As it was, I barely escaped with my life.

Hard by Fishguard are the Prescelly Hills, from which huge blocks of rare bluestone were transported across England to form parts of Stonehenge some 4,000 to 5,000 years ago. How long it took to cut the stones, what tools were used, and how and why they made that long journey – 135 miles (217 km) as the crow flies – are mysteries to this day. But the rarity of these stones, known and recognized all those centuries ago, are thought to have given them a special quality, connected perhaps with religion or with the study of stars.

After running southwards through some of the most sparsely inhabited countryside in Wales, the River Teifi flows through Devil's Bridge, Tregaron, Lampeter (world famous as a training centre for Anglican clergy), Llandyssul and Newcastle Emlyn, finally draining into Cardigan Bay just where it levels out after the long sweep down from Aberystwyth. It passes through a landscape varied between marshland and moorland, as rich in wild-life as anywhere in the country – especially with such rare birds as the peregrine falcon, the golden plover and the almost extinct red kite. Fishermen on the Teifi use the old-fashioned, indeed primeval, but highly efficient coracle for netting the local salmon, while their womenfolk specialize in making delicious laver bread from seaweed.

Mynydd Bodafon is a low range on Anglesey, which is made up of some of Britain's oldest rocks, with some lovely bays and capes, and a wealth of prehistoric relics. It was for centuries the centre of ancient Druid worship and its people fiercely resisted the Romans. Indeed it was while fighting here that the Roman general Suetonius Paulinus received news of Queen Boudicca's revolt and made his famous forced march back to Essex to smash it. Anglesey was also the home of Owen Tudor, grandfather of Henry VII. My wife and I spent a wonderful holiday here in the 1950s at a cottage called 'Clyn Wen' and made the owner an offer for it. But when we found that it was the best part of a seven-hour drive from London to reach it, we gave up the idea.

North Wales

Some time in the 6th century, Saint Seiriol founded a Christian community on Puffin Island (Ynys Seiriol in Welsh) off the north-east tip of Anglesey. Every day he trampled half of the 24 miles (39 km) to confer with his friend Saint Cybi who had built a monastery on the island's south-western tip. Halfway between the two they would meet for a little prayer meeting, followed by a simple hymn, a bite of biscuit and a sip of wine. Sometimes, when a brother died, Cybi would walk the whole way to help Seiriol carry the body over to Puffin Island and lay it to rest.

Wales has many Christian associations, as well as prehistoric relics, standing stones and ancient burial chambers, while between Prestatyn on the northern coast of Clwyd and Chepstow at the mouth of the River Wye is the great trough known as Offa's Dyke. Constructed by the Mercian king Offa, who reigned between AD 757 and 796, this dyke was partly a demarcation line and partly a line of defence. To cross a dyke soldiers had first to run downhill before hazarding the upward clamber. In both cases they were unavoidably vulnerable. But for me, the most moving of all testimonies to the past is still the historic communion between the two humble saints at the end of their 12-mile (19½-km) tramp across Anglesey.

Close to St Seiriol's headquarters stands the magnificent Beaumaris Castle, built by Edward I in 1295 to complete his chain of defences across North Wales. But it was never finished and, therefore, never used. It is thus very much as it was when first built, and an object lesson for students of military history.

A short way from Beaumaris is Thomas Telford's masterpiece, the Menai suspension bridge, one of the finest of its kind anywhere in the world, its twin towers sunk deep at either end, with great cables hanging between them to carry the road from London to

Menai Bridge, Thomas Telford's masterpiece, carries road traffic from the mainland across to Anglesey. Opened in 1826, it is one of the half dozen most beautiful bridges in Britain. Telford was the son of a Scottish shepherd. Apprenticed at the age of 15 to a stone-mason, he early gained a feeling for building, especially in stone, and he showed in a busy life that he could turn his hand to a wide variety of construction work, whether canals (he made Scotland's Great Glen a navigable waterway), roads, bridges (1,200 in Scotland alone), railways, harbours or viaducts. He built the superb St Katharine's Docks in London's East End (now a Maritime Museum) and drew up plans for draining the fenlands of Norfolk. He was one of the self-educated geniuses of Victorian Britain.

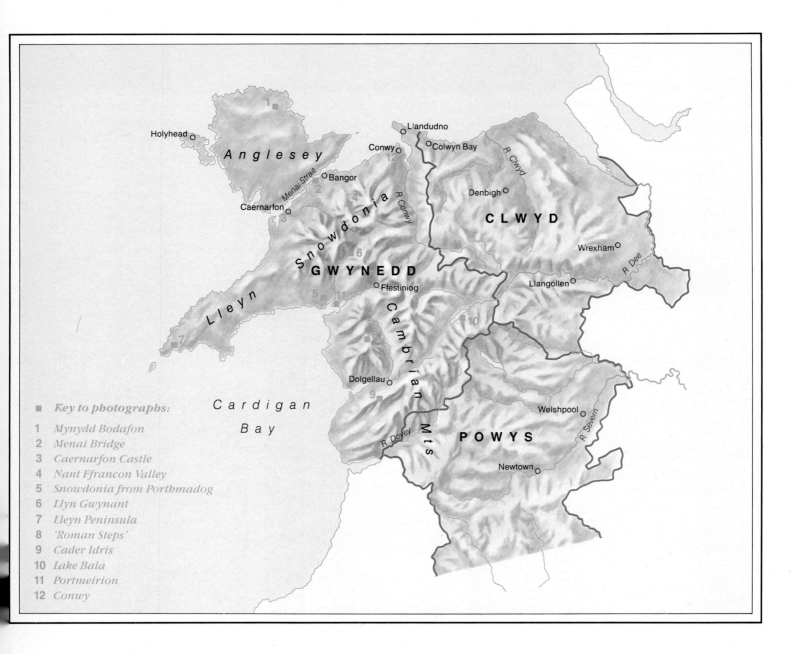

Key to photographs:

1 Mynydd Bodafon
2 Menai Bridge
3 Caernarfon Castle
4 Nant Ffrancon Valley
5 Snowdonia from Porthmadog
6 Llyn Gwynant
7 Lleyn Peninsula
8 'Roman Steps'
9 Cader Idris
10 Lake Bala
11 Portmeirion
12 Conwy

Left: Offa's Dyke is a vast earthwork, 140 miles (225 km) long, which was constructed on the Welsh border by Offa, King of Mercia, some time between AD 784 and 796 as a defensive line against the Celts. It followed the general pattern of the Roman wall which had a ditch and a vallum on its northern side. While running down into the ditch or climbing up towards the defenders, attackers were of necessity highly vulnerable. This awe-inspiring project required human labour on a scale matching that of building the pyramids and, in this case, pursued under a hail of enemy rocks and arrows.

Holyhead. To my mind the most captivating of all the world's bridges are suspended ones, mingling a masculine solidity with voluptuous feminine curves.

A combined road and rail bridge also spans the Menai Strait. The original tubular bridge by Robert Stephenson was completed in 1846, some 20 years later than the suspension bridge, but the tubular structure was destroyed by fire in 1970 and the present bridge built on the surviving brick and stonework.

On the mainland overlooking the Menai Strait is Caernarfon Castle, birthplace of the first Prince of Wales, a title bestowed in 1301 by Edward I upon his ill-fated son who became Edward II, and used as an administrative centre for the government of the whole of North Wales. In recent times the castle was once again brought into service for the investiture of our much-loved Prince Charles.

From the shores of the Menai Strait, the whole glory of Snowdonia National Park stretches away to the south-east, reaching 3,560 feet (1,085 metres) above sea level, the highest peak in Wales, while to the south is the Lleyn Peninsula, one of the country's most precious areas of natural beauty, with South Stack lighthouse planted on its end like a concrete jewel. On the southern coast of the magnificent county of Gwynedd, Harlech Castle calls to mind its long, defiant history and the song 'Men of Harlech' with its rousing tune. Here the greatest of all Welsh heroes, Owen Glendower, held sway at the end of the 14th century and here his heroic son-in-law Edward Mortimer starved to death rather than surrender.

East of Harlech, at the southern end of Snowdonia, stands Cader Idris, Wales's second highest mountain, part of a landscape of true scenic grandeur. Like that of Robin Hood, the legend of King Arthur travelled far and wide, and just as Edinburgh boasts his 'seat', so, here in a fold of the mountains we find his 'chair'.

South of Cader Idris in west-central Wales is Machynlleth, a humble town, but what a glorious page of Welsh history was written here, for it was in Machynlleth that Owen Glendower defied the overweening authority of the English by proclaiming the first independent

Above left: Caernarfon Castle, founded by King Edward I in 1283, was probably intended as a birthday present for his son who was born there the following year and immediately created the first Prince of Wales. It is one of a chain of strongholds known for their advanced design, at the same time acting not only as castles but also as palaces. Caernarfon became the ceremonial capital of Wales and its castle was twice more brought back into service for the investitures of Prince Edward in 1911 and of Prince Charles in 1969. Caernarfon used to be spelt Caernarvon, but in recent years the Welsh have systematically corrected the many spelling mistakes of Welsh place-names perpetrated by English map-makers.

Above: The impressive Nant Ffrancon valley leading to the Nant Ffrancon Pass is one of the highlights of the Snowdonia National Park. In The Pilgrim's Progress John Bunyan's hero Christian climbs the Hill Difficulty. Here we climb up a valley, treading on foundations formed 450 million years ago when this whole area was a group of low-lying volcanic islands surrounded by a shallow sea.

Other rocks later formed over the volcanic ones and recently, in the Ice Age, the whole region was buried by glaciers, and so it is full of rugged mountains, high passes, sheer rock faces and escarpments, steep-sided valleys, forests, lakes and waterfalls. Here is everything nature has to offer except a chance to till the soil.

Welsh parliament with himself as its leader. How brilliantly Shakespeare depicted the struggle between England and Wales in *The First Part of Henry IV* and how superbly he caught the defiant character of Glendower and his belief in witchcraft as an aid to statecraft. Glendower symbolizes all those national heroes who have risked life and limb to bring freedom to their precious homelands.

North-east of Machynlleth and set in a wonderful landscape on the edge of Snowdonia is Lake Bala, Wales's biggest natural stretch of inland water. In former days Bala itself was famous for stockings, hand-knitted by the local women who, in an unofficial way, were appointed 'sole stocking-knitters and purveyors thereof to His Majesty King George III.'

In southern Clwyd, the north-easternmost county of Wales, is one of the country's finest beauty spots, the Vale of Llangollen, known around the world for its International Musical Eisteddfod, but made famous in the later years of the 18th century by three remarkable women, Lady Eleanor Butler, her friend Sarah Ponsonby and their maid-servant Mary Carryl. Their wit, charm and cultivation and the lovely belongings with which they filled their magnificent half-timbered home, Plas Newydd, attracted many celebrities to visit them, including William Wordsworth, Robert Southey and the Duke of Wellington.

St Asaph in northern Clwyd is little more than a

Previous spread: This distant view of Snowdonia was taken at the Causeway across the River Glaslyn at Porthmadog, often spelt Portmadoc. This area is clustered with attractive villages and delightful sandy beaches. The charming Lleyn peninsula stretches away to the west, with the resort of Pwllheli, one of Wales's loveliest villages, Abersoch, and a few miles farther on Aberdaron, where there is a view of Bardsey Island, visited by millions of sea birds. Legend tells us that the wizard Merlin, who arranged for the birth of King Arthur, lies buried on this island.

Above left: Llyn Gwynant is about 3 miles (5 km) north-east of Bedgellert, in the heart of Snowdonia. Legend has it that Gelert was a fine greyhound belonging to Llewellyn the Great. One day when the prince called him, he failed to come. On his return Gelert, spattered with blood, greeted the prince. Llewellyn rushed to his baby son's bedroom. Bloodstained bedclothes lay around and, thinking that Gelert had killed his precious son, he plunged his sword into the dog's heart. As Gelert breathed his last, Llewellyn's son crawled out from under the cradle-clothes. Then outside the bedroom Llewellyn saw the body of a huge wolf which the faithful Gelert had killed while defending the baby. The heart-broken Prince vowed that his castle and the village around it should be named after Gelert. This tale expresses the fiercely loyal character of the Welsh and their strong attachment to their legends.

Above: Porth Iago on the Lleyn peninsula is one of the secluded spots that a family likes to find. Shielded from the weather by Ireland and warmed by the Gulf Stream, this area of natural beauty is more like Devonshire than Wales. It contains many prehistoric remains, especially the cluster of Iron Age hut circles in the north-west, and the island of Bardsey in the south has echoes of early Christians who lived and died there. I imagine the early saints had one deep sense which most of us lack, the sense of being alone, the certainty that time was short and that they must prepare themselves for eternity with their finest prayers and psalms. This was just the place for a quiet chat and a surprise visit from the Master: 'Come in, dear Lord, and break a little crust with us.' And the Lord Jesus would enter.

195

Top: The so-called Roman Steps, above Cwm Bychan near Harlech, are
certainly not Roman in origin. The Romans were indeed in Wales and they
had master-masons and stone-carvers of the highest order. Their stone-work
fell a long way short of the Greek ideal, but not on the technical level, and
any Roman who produced steps like these would have lost his job. Perhaps
they were made from stone left over from the building of Harlech Castle in
1283 or fragments of ashlar knocked off by the siege guns of Owen
Glendower. More likely still a bright local grasped the fact that north-
western Wales would all too soon become one of Britain's most popular
tourist areas and the more 'history' you could add to it the more attractive
it would be.

196

Left: Cader Idris, near Dolgellau in southern Gwynedd, is one of the highest mountains in Wales. It is a volcanic massif shaped by glaciers, which have left behind tarns in hollows called cwms in Welsh. Like so many features of Wales, there is a rather Greek-like legend about the mountain, to the effect that anyone who sleeps on its summit will wake up either blind or mad or a poet. Homer, the greatest poet of antiquity, was blind; and William Blake, second only to Shakespeare in my own Pantheon, was mad. So the Welsh legend should not deter aspirants for the laurel crown from taking a chance!

Lake Bala is the biggest natural lake in Wales, with Arthurian associations like Wales in general. One of the finest collections of Arthurian legends is the Mabinogion, written in Welsh and translated by Lady Charlotte Guest. In one of its most mysterious stories, Arthur's favourite page awakens one night with a scream. He dreamed he had stolen one of the golden altar candlesticks from the Chapel Perilous. A knight in black armour caught up with him as he rode away, tore the candlestick from his jerkin and then stabbed him. When Arthur and Lancelot turned the boy over, there was a dagger in his side.

197

village, but it boasts Britain's smallest cathedral, founded in the 6th century. The north coast of Wales contains a number of attractive seaside resorts, the most popular being Llandudno; and Conway, whose impressive castle guarded the vulnerable northern end of the Principality, a kind of stone shutter letting the English into Wales, while trying to keep the Welsh out of England. In the end it proved incapable of fulfilling either function. The Welsh gained access to England by sheer talent, willpower and charm, as businessmen, soldiers, footballers, singers and actors, while the English found the pure beauty of

Wales (and its coal and other resources) irresistible.

Looking back on my childhood and the sing-songs we used to have at home with my mother at the piano and my father playing his home-made fiddle, it seems strange that some of the most popular items were about the countries England had failed to bash into submission. From Scotland there were 'The Bonnie, Bonnie Banks of Loch Lomond', 'Annie Laurie' and 'Afton Water'; from Ireland 'The Dear Little Shamrock' and 'The Mountains of Mourne'; and from Wales 'Men of Harlech' and 'Land of my Fathers', which neither my father nor any of his forefathers had ever set eyes on or were ever likely to.

Above left: Portmeirion, Gwynedd, is an Italianate village created by architect Clough Williams-Ellis at the north end of Tremadog Bay. It is usually described as a 'folly'. The Oxford English Dictionary defines 'folly' as 'a costly structure that is considered useless', but Portmeirion, whose construction began in 1926, is neither useless nor was ever considered so. It incorporates a luxury hotel, terraced gardens filled with rare flowers, cypress and palm trees, a slim four-tiered Campanile and a little private castle. Instead of 'folly' we should say 'flight of fancy'.

Above: Conway, or Conwy as the Welsh spell it, is in north-eastern Gwynedd. Its castle, shown here from the landward side, is another formidable strong-point in Edward I's conquest of Wales. What castles he built! The walls were 15 feet (4.6 metres) thick – pace that out on your garden path – and every inch of them was covered by the defenders. Earlier in this book I spoke of abbot and surveyor putting their heads together over the Ely Lantern. By the same token we can imagine Edward drawing his conception of the perfect castle on a piece of vellum for the army of stone-masons employed on the job. Nowhere else in Britain are Edward's castles matched for strength and defensive arrangement. But within a few years the invention of cannon had rendered them obsolete.

Neidpath Castle, near Peebles on the River Tweed, is in the Borders Region which offers attractive scenery, a superb agricultural tradition and a wealth of historic buildings. But the Borders is hardly counted as Scotland at all by some Scots who speak of its inhabitants as 'Borderers'. For centuries there was no settled frontier between England and Scotland. Neither in language, landscape, mode of life nor history did southern Scotland differ from northern England. Nevertheless the Borders has played a classic role in history as a priceless buffer zone, taking the first shock of all the assaults by the English. In fact the only major battle ever fought in the Highlands was Culloden in 1745. It resulted in the Clans – the very soul of Scotland – being crushed and rendered powerless.

Lowland Scotland

For many years a skeleton lay hidden in our family cupboard. My mother had been born in Scotland, but we never knew precisely where until, in 1973, I received a letter from an old lady living in Castle Douglas, south-west of Dumfries. She said that as a child she had known my mother and that she 'came from Glenlochar only a few miles from here. She was a love child and when still quite young was farmed out to a family in the south and so far as I know never returned'. So that was the family secret, and what an innocent one!

A year later, returning from a trip to Glasgow, I decided to visit this village where I felt I partly belonged. Suddenly there it was, the River Dee, the bridge, the great house set among a forest of birch trees, and the school. The teacher Mrs McDowell welcomed me in to see the room in which my mother had learned her ABC a hundred years ago. Can you wonder that I found it hard to keep back the tears? 'Now', said Mrs McDowell' 'we only have seven pupils and they cost more than £2,000 a year to educate, each one of them. So next term the school will close.' I had come just in time.

South-western Scotland, with its rich farmland, is largely unspoiled because it lies safe and sound off the main line from Glasgow to London. West of Castle Douglas is the superb Glen Trool Forest Park and north of this scenic wilderness is Alloway, birthplace of Robert Burns, Scotland's national poet. While Burns was setting down immortal songs like 'Auld Lang Syne', 'Ye Banks and Braes of Bonnie Doon' and 'Afton Water' (to say nothing of great poems like 'Tam O'Shanter' and 'Holy Willie's Prayer'), the English had not yet torn themselves free from the satiric chains of the heroic couplet. Besides, Burns wrote in his native dialect, not caring to ape the strains of Received Standard English as it was one day to be called.

Above: Jedburgh Abbey is one of a cluster of magnificent ruins, which also include Dryburgh, Kelso and Melrose, in the south-eastern corner of the Borders region. Jedburgh Abbey dates from 1118, only 52 years after the Battle of Hastings, but the semi-circular arch had already taken over and here, despite the ravaging by English invaders, you can see it at its very finest.

Left: This was Sir Walter Scott's favourite view of his homeland, a fine vista of the River Tweed flowing through a lush and verdant landscape. Scott (1771–1832) was born in Edinburgh, but the Borders was a major source of inspiration. He wrote with great speed and his output, both of prose and verse, was prodigious. His stories served the prime purpose of drawing attention to the beauties of his beloved homeland, which was until then little appreciated.

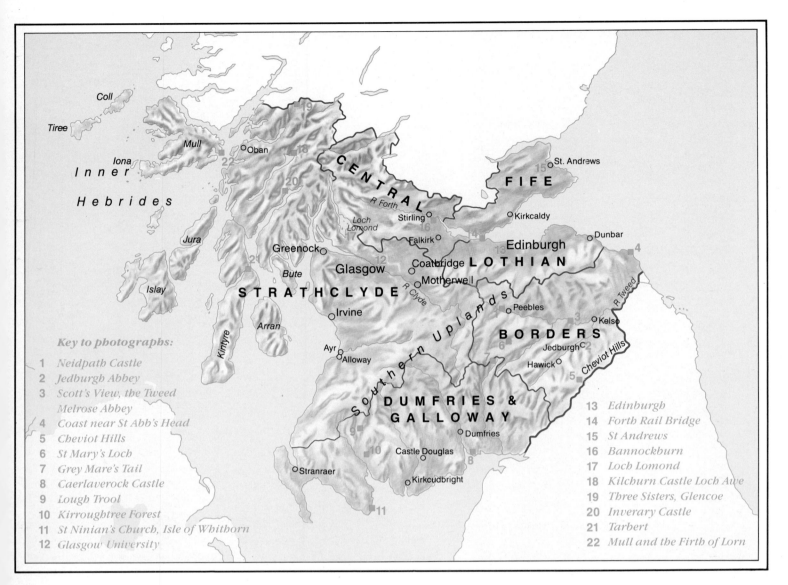

Key to photographs:

1 Neidpath Castle
2 Jedburgh Abbey
3 Scott's View, the Tweed
  Melrose Abbey
4 Coast near St Abb's Head
5 Cheviot Hills
6 St Mary's Loch
7 Grey Mare's Tail
8 Caerlaverock Castle
9 Lough Trool
10 Kirroughtree Forest
11 St Ninian's Church, Isle of Whithorn
12 Glasgow University

13 Edinburgh
14 Forth Rail Bridge
15 St Andrews
16 Bannockburn
17 Loch Lomond
18 Kilchurn Castle Loch Awe
19 Three Sisters, Glencoe
20 Inverary Castle
21 Tarbert
22 Mull and the Firth of Lorn

Following spread: Melrose Abbey, shattered as it is, shows the transitional style at its sweetest and lightest. It was occupied by Cistercian monks from Rievaulx in North Yorkshire which explains why its feeling is so similar. The English destroyed Melrose in 1543 as part of Henry VIII's campaign to break up the monastic system. I would hazard a guess that the English have destroyed more religious houses than any other people. Of the 1,000 or so monasteries, abbeys and convents flourishing in 1500, not a single one remains intact. It is a fierce record. But as Robert Browning wrote in Abt Vogler: 'On the earth the broken arcs; in the heaven, a perfect round.' At least let us hope so!

East of Castle Douglas is Gretna, famous for the blacksmith's shop where couples were once wedded without bans or licence. Gretna served thousands of true lovers escaping from uncomprehending parents and it claimed that bonds sealed over its anvil bound firmer and lasted longer than any others.

East of Gretna is the Borders region with its cluster of ruined abbeys – Dryburgh, Jedburgh, Kelso and Melrose – despoiled and desecrated either by the English in their long and unsuccessful attempt to subdue the Scots, or by local bandits wreaking havoc wherever they got a chance. But all four embody some of the finest examples of Gothic architecture in the land. A few miles from this group of abbeys is Abbotsford, home of Sir Walter Scott, who is buried in the abbey at Dryburgh. It was while taking a morning walk in the fields near his home and seeing the new-born lambs skipping about in the sunshine that he exclaimed: 'Aren't they lovely?' 'Yes,' replied his highly practical wife, 'with mint sauce.'

Like Ireland and Wales, Scotland is to the English a foreign country inhabited by a foreign people, boasting a vast untamed wilderness in the north and, in the west, a

Right: This stretch of coast near St Abb's Head is in the north-eastern part of the Borders Region. The lighthouse at St Abb's Head flashes six times every minute and can be seen for 20 miles (32 km), a necessary precaution on a coast as treacherous as this. A little way to the north is the ruined Fast Castle, used by Sir Walter Scott as the prototype of the Tower of Edgar of Ravenswood in his The Bride of Lammermuir. My Scottish aunts never read Scott's book on Sundays, nor would they let us read them, because they were novels and novels were wicked. They also wouldn't let us whistle. So you see what I have had to live down.

Below: The Cheviot Hills, straddling the English-Scottish border, are like a giant taking a well-earned nap under a warm coverlet of Mother Earth. Beneath this coverlet lies an ancient dome of lava that burst through in the early Devonian period, nearly 400 million years ago. The weathering of the lava and other rocks has produced rich soil as can be seen in the overlapping furrows waiting to burst into full glory of spring and summer corn. There are not only crops, but also fine Cheviot sheep with their tough fleece; and don't forget the incomparable Border collie!

pattern of islands even more beautiful than those of Greece. Scotsmen wear kilts and their women plaids as freely as the English sport public school and regimental ties. And they do so for the same reason. Tartan and tie are both marks of heritage, of attachment to history, of unbroken and unbreakable loyalties. They record glorious achievements on the battlefield, on the football pitch, in the financial market-place, in science and in medicine. Scotland has bred great men in all fields of human endeavour and, not least, extending over many centuries, a fierce opposition to the English. By the time I was ten years old I knew of William Wallace and of Robert the Bruce and his spider. And even the hard-boiled English learned to blush at the mention of Bloody Cumberland.

Scotland is rich in battlefields and the glory won on them, whether in victory or defeat. Flodden, Culloden, Stirling, Falkirk, Bannockburn and Prestonpans are all names which cannot fail to stir the heart. And for two

Above: St Mary's Loch is in what once was the county of Selkirkshire. Selkirk itself has a museum which contains a flag captured by local soldiers who were shoemakers, or 'soutars' in civilian life. The soutars must have been busy in 1745, for as everyone knows, care of the feet is the decisive factor in soldiering. This raises the question of how 5,000 to 6,000 Highlanders marched over rough tracks from northern Scotland into England and back again. I scarcely believe the suggestion that they wrapped their feet in deerskin. More likely, local people made presents of their own footwear and the soldiers must have bought footwear en route and recruited as many soutars as they could. An army without boots is unthinkable.

Caerlaverock Castle, on the Solway Firth 6 miles (10 km) south-west of Dumfries, was built in about 1290 of local sandstone, which is useless against siege artillery – another example of a castle built without taking account of recent developments in defence. Ten miles (6 km) north-east of Caerlaverock is Ecclefechan, birthplace of the historian and critic Thomas Carlyle (1795–1881), whose home is now preserved as a museum, while to the west are the ruins of Sweetheart Abbey, founded in the 13th century by Devorguila, wife of Scotland's vassal king John Balliol.

centuries, Scottish Highlanders have stood in the forefront of British armies all over the world – Black Watch, Gordon Highlanders, Scots and Coldstream Guards, Highland Light Infantry, Queen's Own Scottish Borderers and others. Someone once ventured to define Highlanders as 'killers'. 'No sir,' replied Dr Johnson, 'they are men who offer themselves to be killed.'

North of the Borders region is Lothian and Edinburgh, Scotland's capital and one of the most beautiful cities in Europe. Built on the remains of an extinct volcano, it is a city of high culture and academic achievement. It is also rich in Scottish history – many houses along the Royal Mile were built in the 16th and 17th centuries, and the oldest part of its castle dates back nearly 900 years. In St Giles's Cathedral John Knox, the

Below: *The 200-foot (61-metre) high Grey Mare's Tail is a lovely cascade 6 miles (10 km) north-east of Moffat in the Dumfries and Galloway Region. Moffat is a sheep-farming centre, proclaiming the fact by a statue of a ram in the middle of its high street – just as Thirsk in North Yorkshire has a fully equipped bull as the trademark of its senior public house. Moffat became a popular resort in the mid-17th century when water from the local spring was found to have therapeutic value, and many distinguished visitors came here for treatment, including Robert Burns, who is said to have written one of his jolliest songs, 'Willie Brew'd a Peck o' Maut', here.*

Bottom: *Loch Trool in Glen Trool is one of the scenic highlights of south-western Scotland. This enchanting region has lochs and waterfalls, a lovely coastline, grassy uplands where the hardy Galloway cattle browse, and peaks rising north of Loch Trool to 2,766 feet (843 metres) at Merrick, the highest mountain in the south-west, confirming the region's claim to be called the Alps of South-West Scotland. Robert the Bruce held out among these hills, 'among these barren crags', during his years as a fugitive. Here in this 'lost' corner of Scotland the Covenanters were hunted down and slaughtered for daring to question established beliefs.*

Left: St Ninian's Church is on the Isle of Whithorn, south of Wigtown. Pilgrims once rested here on their way to the Saint's shrine. Ninian was the son of a local chieftain who went to Rome in around AD 385 and came back to Scotland to convert the Picts. He built himself a little shrine at the southern tip of The Machars peninsula and here in this church pilgrims could rest before tramping the last few miles to the shrine. Around the corner on the west side of the peninsula is a tiny cave in which Ninian sought refuge, I imagine, from being suffocated by pilgrims.

Below: Horses haul timber in Kirroughtree Forest, probably for pit props somewhere up Glasgow way. The horses are local Clydesdales, Scotland's giant work-horses. The props are loaded on a sledge, a primitive but effective mode of transport. Hardly any lifting is required, because they can be rolled into position. I wonder how many people ever think of the pit props still underground that have played a crucial role in heating their homes. And how many miners' wives remember that the pit props keep their menfolk alive?

If I was asked to select a photograph which embodied the spirit of Glasgow, most of my friends would expect me to choose a picture of the Clyde, with gantries, cranes and dockyard maties hard at work doing the job they do so magnificently amid the smoke and fire of a shipyard. But Glasgow has much besides that. To begin with it has a fine university, shown here, and a set of straight-from-the-shoulder values unsurpassed in Britain. Leaving aside the achievement of its engineers, especially Thomas Telford, the greatest of the great, Scotland's primal claim is, in my view, the creation of a truly national theatre. It is at once home-grown but of international quality and scope, with the advantage of having its own native dialect – which makes it national in the true sense unlike London's National Theatre, which should really be called 'The International Theatre'.

celebrated Calvinist and author of *The First Blast of the Trumpet against the Monstrous Regiment of Women*, preached some of his fiercest sermons.

In Holyroodhouse are the private apartments of Mary Queen of Scots and we shudder to think that here was committed one of history's most brutal murders, that of the Queen's devoted secretary David Rizzio, whom her husband Darnley suspected of being her lover.

For three weeks in late summer Edinburgh mounts A Festival of Music and Drama, chosen from among the finest talent in the world and leavened with fringe events on a humbler, but often no less brilliant a scale. At the first of these festivals, in 1948, I had the honour of playing Christopher Sly in the Old Vic's production of Shakespeare's *The Taming of the Shrew* and in 1983 the aged manservant Firs in Chekhov's *The Cherry Orchard*. On that second trip I paid a visit to the new Forth Bridge connecting Lothian with Fife. This structure would have warmed the heart of Thomas Telford even more than it did mine, and he died with over 1,200 bridges to his credit, in Scotland alone.

211

Below: Where do we begin a rapid overview of the great city of Edinburgh? In Princes Street, the castle, Salisbury Crags, Arthur's Seat, Holyroodhouse, St Giles Cathedral, the Royal Mile, Lauriston House, Parliament House, Greyfriars Church? Like most of Europe's ancient cities, Edinburgh is composed of a series of historical layers, representing Picts, Romans, Saxons, Vikings, Normans and so on, like peeling off the pages from a drawing block. It's all there, 2,000 to 3,000 years of Scottish history. The history of every old city is unique, each one is the testimony, the seal and certificate of the city's identity. And if you put all these identities together, they add up to the personality of the country. For Scotland's you could start at no better place than here in the country's lovely capital.

Right: The Forth Rail Bridge is seen here from North Queensferry. Built between 1883 and 1890, it links Lothian and Fife. It has two main spans with the rocky Inchgarvae Island in the middle. It was a great achievement for its period and for its immense length of 1.55 miles (2.5 km). Its slightly over-sturdy appearance is perhaps accounted for by the fact that in 1879 the 2.5-mile (4-km) long bridge over the River Tay collapsed during a gale when a passenger train was passing over it. More than 70 people died.

Above: St Andrews is an ancient city north of Edinburgh, just around the corner of Fife Ness. The city, truly one of the great names in the intellectual life of Europe, has Scotland's oldest university, founded in 1411 and so treading hard upon England's Oxford and Cambridge. In the early days, most of the studies would have been concerned with Latin, Greek, Divinity, Philosophy and a little Mathematics – 'how many angels can stand on the point of a needle?' If you got it wrong you could easily burn. St Andrews is also a popular resort and has a ruined cathedral 800 years old and a castle destroyed in 1547.

Left: A statue of Robert the Bruce overlooks the field of Bannockburn where, in 1314, an English army, three times the size of the Scottish force, was routed and put to flight. The English were badly led, for Edward I had died and his inefficient, luxury-loving son was no match for Bruce who had spent years fighting guerrilla actions, studying and thinking day and night about the techniques of warfare, especially the use of the bow and arrrow. Bruce was the first leader to plant a solid bank of archers on either side of his infantry, so that it could not be enveloped by enemy cavalry, an example followed by British commanders for the next 300 years.

On the Fife coast is the city of St Andrews, once Scotland's ecclesiastical capital, whose university vies with the world's greatest in fame and high achievement. But St Andrews is even more famous as the headquarters of Scotland's favourite pastime, the Royal and Ancient game of golf. St Andrews is to golf what Lords is to cricket. And the magnificent course at Carnoustie is only a few miles away across the Firth of Tay.

In west-central Scotland we open our arms to the roaring life of Glasgow. Here we meet the Scots at their greatest, waging war against iron and steel and bending them to their unbreakable will. Not that its people are by nature belligerent, but that when faced with the brutal challenge of the Industrial Revolution they met it with an unmatched mingling of muscle, pride, skill and humour. The list of ocean-going liners built on Clydeside –

including the ill-fated *Lusitania*, the *Queen Mary* and both the *Elizabeths* in the passenger field, and warships *Repulse*, *Renown*, *Vanguard*, *Barham*, *Kelvin*, *Ardent*, *Acasta* and scores of others – give Glasgow pride of place among the industrial aristocracy. But like Birmingham, Bradford and Newcastle, Glasgow has managed (but only just) to contain its sprawl of shipyard and factory. A short ride from the city centre brings you to a wide range of glorious countryside: Campsie Fells, Kilpatrick Hills, the Trossachs, the Kyles of Bute and, loveliest of all, world-famous Loch Lomond.

Possibly to escape from the pressures of life in London, or the wish to build up his depleted bank balance, the great actor Edmund Kean (1787–1833) purchased a cottage on the Isle of Bute in the Firth of Clyde and, when the fancy took him, would travel those 700 miles (1,300 km) there and the same distance back, to refresh himself with the keen air of the island and doubtless with drams of the fine local whisky.

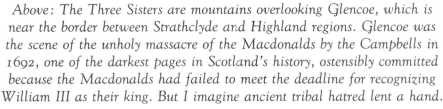

Above: The Three Sisters are mountains overlooking Glencoe, which is near the border between Strathclyde and Highland regions. Glencoe was the scene of the unholy massacre of the Macdonalds by the Campbells in 1692, one of the darkest pages in Scotland's history, ostensibly committed because the Macdonalds had failed to meet the deadline for recognizing William III as their king. But I imagine ancient tribal hatred lent a hand.

Above: Kilchurn Castle is a lovely ruin built in 1440 on the north shore of Loch Awe, with Ben Cruichan rising to 3,689 feet (1,124 metres) in the background. The loch contains several islands, including Inishail, headquarters of an early Christian settlement whose ruined chapel and cemetery can still be seen. Why do we like ruins? I suppose we like to imagine all the life and activity that has gone on inside them and how they can hold genuine conversations with us, about our origins and past history.

Following spread: Inverary Castle was built in 1770, 25 years after the collapse of Bonnie Prince Charlie's attempt to recapture the kingdom for his family. The clans were disarmed and put under severe restrictions. Castle-building was a thing of the past. Here a London-based designer, Robert Adam (a Classicist to his fingertips), worked with a local man Bob Milne to create something in the Scottish baronial style, using blue-green chlorite slate and topping off the flanking turrets with cones.

Tarbert is a fishing village at the north end of Loch Tarbert which cuts between Knapdale and Kintyre. Just north of the village is Tarbert Castle, one of the strongholds of Robert the Bruce. Here one catches the savage quality of medieval Scottish life, because there are eight castles within this little rugged area – eight family feuds, with every man's hand against everyone else's.

Forty miles (64 km) a day by coach was good going in those days, so it must have taken the best part of two weeks to get there and two weeks to get back. Allowing for a month's stay on the island, this would take up the whole eight weeks of the summer recess. Probably far longer, for his national fame would lure him to give performances en route, playing to packed houses and demanding a good cut at the box office, at such centres as Bury St Edmunds, York and Carlisle. We know that he carried a complete wardrobe with him, for during his stay

on the island he would dress up as some of his favourite characters, including King Lear, Hamlet, Othello and Sir Giles Overreach, and spend part of the day holding court among his island retainers. You can still see Kean's cottage and the four stone pillars he built to carry decorative iron gates at the entrance to his estate. The pillars were surmounted by the sculptured heads of four great figures in theatrical history: Shakespeare, Philip Massinger, David Garrick and who else fourth but himself, Edmund Kean!

This view shows the Firth of Lorn and Mull, one of the loveliest islands of the Inner Hebrides, with mainland Strathclyde behind us. Mull is not only to be savoured for its scenery, but it is also famous in history from having tiny Iona tacked on to its south-western end. Here St Columba, sailing from Ireland, made his landfall in AD 563. And from here he set out to convert the Picts.

Skara Brae, a Stone Age village on the Orkney Islands, is anything between 2,500 and 4,000 years old. It is a group of dwellings connected by passageways and tunnels, the whole roofed over with fir boughs and bracken. The fire in the central fireplace was made by drilling dead leaves with a piece of wood to make a flame. Fish caught in the shallows were baked, unless you preferred them raw. Most of the family slept on mattresses of gorse and seaweed on surrounding shelves. Their bed coverlets and clothes were made of animal skin stitched together with fish-bone needles. A small people – the average height of a male was 4 feet 7 inches (1.4 metres) – they had no doctors, no names, no language and no god. But they had souls, so the appearance and reappearance of the Sun and Moon were reassuring and dead relatives were placed in the earth with heavy stones to mark the spots. There were plenty of houses like these all over Britain.

Northern Scotland

A physical map of Scotland shows an unruly mass of mountains and valleys as if, after the huge act of Creation, the Almighty had found in His hand some remnants of the primal clay and carelessly flung them down with a sigh of relief that the job was finished. For this is a wilderness, dangerous and beautiful, untamed and untamable, still marked by the hand of God, still bearing his signature.

And lying off its northern shore are two final ragged fistsful of that clay, the Orkneys and Shetlands, almost bare of trees, windswept, waveswept, the edge of creation, *ultima Thule*. Britain's Cockleshell heroes of the Second World War, using all the technology of the 20th century, performed miracles of seamanship around these northern isles. But what kind of men, dressed in what kind of garb and navigating what kind of craft settled on this cluster of islands 5,000 years ago. Take a trip to Skara Brae on the west coast of Mainland, the biggest island in the Orkneys, and think it over. Here you stand inside part of an early housing estate, similar to Chysauster in Cornwall, except that here the estate was found almost intact, not only foundations, but also walls, doorways, alleyways and the very best that the Stone Age had to offer in the way of furniture, beds, shelves, cupboards and storerooms, all made of stone.

In the Orkneys and Shetlands is a rich store of evidence of our long journey from the Stone Age through the Bronze and Iron ages upwards to the Norman arch and pillar seen at their very finest in Kirkwall, whose red and yellow stone cathedral is one of the treasures of British architecture. In 1960 the skull of Orkney's King Magnus, murdered by a rival in 1115, perhaps for having embraced Christianity so ardently, was found inside one of the cathedral's columns. It had been split as with an axe, just as his death is described in one of the Norse

sagas. The Norsemen had not yet forgiven their fellow countrymen for having betrayed the old ramshackle pantheon of Scandinavian gods in favour of Christianity.

In 1912, long before the outbreak of the First World War, the renowned First Lord of the Admiralty Jackie Fisher, aided by Winston Churchill, realized that if war came Britain had to find a safe anchorage for its precious Home Fleet, and they chose Scapa Flow, Orkney's great central expanse of sea which could hold with ease 500 or 600 ships and all their shore-based services. And this huge expanse of water served the same noble purpose throughout the second great conflict.

In 1944, just before the invasion of Europe, my old friend John Mills and I got together a revue called *All Adrift* and along with our wives, a dancer and a pianist, took it up to Scapa and performed it all round the

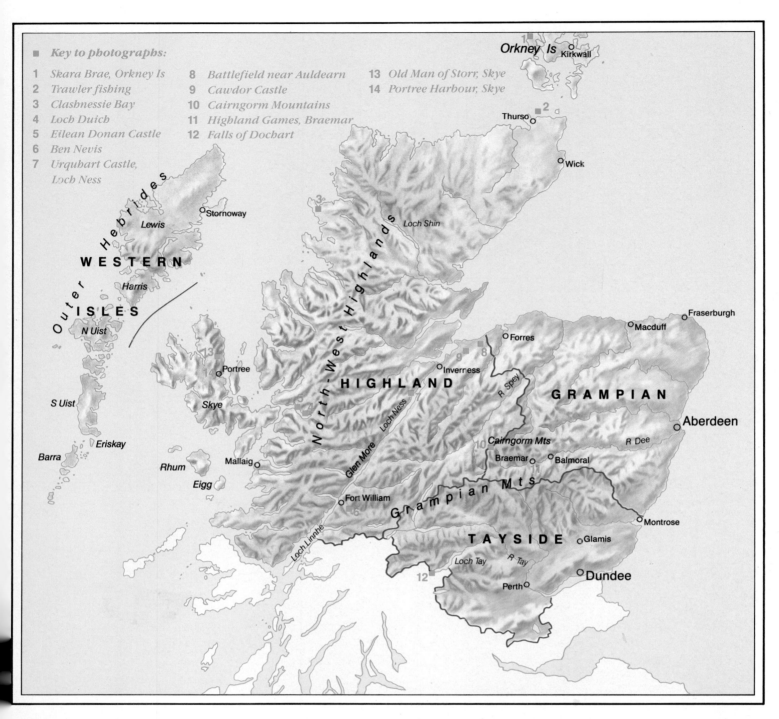

Above left: A Shetland islander knits with new-spun wool. Forty years ago, the Shetlands had few shops so the islanders made almost everything for themselves – petticoats edged with homemade lace, bodices, blouses, skirts, jerseys, stockings, gloves, cloaks, overcoats – everything except boots and shoes which came from the mainland.

They spun their own wool and invented patterned neckbands. About the only thing they did not make was the cambric for petticoats and drawers, but otherwise the women did it all: blanket-stitch, slip-stitch, back-stitch, over-sewing, button-holing and embroidered initialling.

anchorage in whatever space we could find for such a welcome diversion, either afloat or ashore. One song I wrote endeavoured to express the desperation of ships' companies waiting for D-Day. An ordinary seaman addresses a heartfelt query to the Admiralty:

'What about a few days leave eh, First Lord?
What about a few days leave?
You're in Whitehall, you're all right,
Home to the missis and the kids each night,
Lunch with an admiral, supper with a Wren,
But don't forget the bleedin' ships are full of bleedin'
   men.
And dear First Lord, we're getting very bored
So what about a few days leave?'

Whenever I sang this it was greeted with a roar of approval, not least by King George who came to Scapa to

Right: A trawler fishes for herring off northern Scotland. The herring fleet works over pre-selected areas, with two boats pulling between them a trawl, a special net designed to sweep the water between them. When the fleet puts into port with its catch, women skilled in gutting are waiting ready to get to work, sending them off to be smoked over a wood fire. As an island nation, Britain has always relied on the sea for food – cod, crab, halibut, lobster, pilchards, plaice, salmon bass, sole and especially herring. Herring can be treated in many ways: smoked, soused, bloatered or kippered. My favourite is kippers well fried, with brown bread and butter and good strong tea.

Right: Clashnessie Bay in north-western Scotland is wide open to the north wind. The landscape is a foretaste of what awaits you as you travel down the west coast until you reach the far south-west where there is a self-respecting coastline. The north-western coast is ragged, rugged, dishevelled, disorderly, deeply trenched by glaciers with mountains rising straight up out of the lochs, and the sea littered with islands like the aftermath of a long battle between the forces of nature in which the land has put up a titanic struggle and only just survived. The only way to get a full picture of north-western Scotland is by sea. Hire a suitable craft at Stranraer in the south-west and take a three-month cruise.

Left: This oil rig in the Ninian Field of the North Sea is a floating factory where everything must be brought from the mainland – food and drink to satisfy 200 big and hungry men, fresh crewmen, medical supplies, newspapers and letters from home. The murderously rough work is broken into long shifts – two weeks on and two weeks off. The first oil strike in the North Sea was made in the 1950s. Till then Britain's whole complex industrial life had depended on the goodwill of Middle Eastern countries and the United States.

salute his Navy and wish them God speed in the perilous enterprise they were about to undertake.

A few days later we dined on the flagship with General Montgomery and he asked John and me whether we had any comments to make on a speech we had heard him deliver that same afternoon. When we hesitated he said: 'Come on now. You actor Johnnies know all about speaking. I'm only a soldier.' A touch of true humbleness behind his awe-inspiring confidence.

A splendid way to get a bird's eye view of the Scottish Highlands is to sit in the right-hand window seat or stand in the corridor of a railway carriage travelling south from Thurso along the eastern edge of the map,

Left: Eilean Donan Castle stands on an island near the meeting place of three lochs – Loch Alsh, Loch Long and Loch Duich. To me the castle looks vulnerable from all sides. But castle building, like monastery building, was a sign of status. I am no expert, but this seems a perfect example of the amateur approach compared with the highly developed destructive sense of that great castle-builder Edward I. After a chequered career as a castle, Eilean Donan has ended up as a clan war memorial and museum.

Below left: At the eastern end of Loch Duich, a sea inlet tucked into the mainland opposite Skye, are the impressive Five Sisters of Kintail. Loch Duich is joined to Loch Alsh and the Kyle of Lochalsh, where ferries run to Skye, that island whose name is inseparable from that of Bonnie Prince Charlie and his glorious but quite insane attempt to restore the Stuart family to the throne of Britain.

Right: Ben Nevis, Britain's highest mountain at 4,406 feet (1,343 metres), has a rounded summit created by lava flowing through fissures in the rocks, like a saucepan full of porridge boiling over. Its lower slopes are made of granite. The whole glorious mass is bolstered all around by lovely hills, trying with all their might to look like mountains. At its foot is Fort William, one of the strongholds garrisoned by British troops to hold Scotland down. This was Bonnie Prince Charlie's last stop on the way back before the massacre at Culloden. I wonder how many times he said to his staff officers: 'If only you hadn't persuaded me to turn back at Carlisle.' And he may have been right. We shall never know.

Urquhart Castle, one of Scotland's biggest castles, overlooks Loch Ness. This looks like another castle built in a marvellous setting but in the wrong place militarily, because it can be assaulted from rising ground behind and by landings on its two flanks. From its turrets, however, you could keep a constant watch on the loch in the hope of catching a glimpse of its monster. We don't really know if there is such a creature. In any case it will not be a fairy-tale monster, but some survivor from prehistoric times which has managed to stay out of the clutches of mankind in the depths of the black waters of the loch. Such wonders do happen. Nature still has many surprises in store for us.

because that was the only place a railway could be put, so steep and forbidding is the mountain landscape to the west. And what a landscape it is! Through Caithness, Sutherland, Ross and Cromarty before we reach Inverness at the northern end of the Great Glen, famous for Thomas Telford's Caledonian Canal which took him 44 years to build and which turned the glens' string of narrow lakes into a complete navigable waterway. If you make a detour along the Great Glen, you are passing along a huge fissure which once separated the land masses to the north and south. Along this huge rift is Loch Ness whose monster stubbornly fails to surface, while at the far end is Fort William, nestling at the foot of Britain's highest mountain, Ben Nevis.

Turning east from Inverness along the north of the Grampians and the scenic Cairngorms, we suddenly see a signpost that rings a bell. Cawdor. Is this not a word we

learned at school? A few miles farther on is another one. Forres. We consult our map. Forty miles (64 km) farther east lies Macduff. Then the penny drops. We are in Macbeth country. Shakespeare's horrible study of evil is not simply a flight of the imagination but an account of genuine events in ancient Scottish history. And about 80 miles (129 km) to the south, in Tayside, is Glamis, a more recent castle planted on the site of a ruder and more sinister one – perhaps a mere broch – and still the home of royalty, for this is the home of the Queen Mother and birthplace of Princess Margaret. Then come Scone where Malcolm was to be crowned, then Birnham, Dunsinane, Fife, Angus and Menteith. All are here.

Then comes the question. How did Queen Victoria come to choose Balmoral as a royal retreat? Did she know and secretly love her Shakespeare? More likely *Macbeth* was one of Prince Albert's favourite plays, learned at the

This area, near Auldearn which is south-east of Nairn, was the scene of a battle in 1645. The trouble began when, in 1638, Charles I tried to enforce on Scotland the English Prayer Book. He met fierce resistance north of the border. In 1639 an Edinburgh woman, Jenny Geddes, stood up in St Giles Cathedral and threw a stool at the bishop when he started reading the lesson in the English fashion. The stool missed, but the incident led to a general revolt and the signing of what was called the Solemn League and Covenant, binding its signatories to the traditional Presbyterian form of worship. The Covenanters, as they were called, raised an army of some 5,000 men but were routed by the Royalists here in 1645.

231

feet of his German tutors as part of his preparation for marrying an English princess and perhaps it was he who persuaded the Queen that here among the wild Grampians she would be close to some of the deepest roots of her kingdom's history, from Viking times onwards to later Scottish kings ruling from nearby Perth. A brief investigation confirms that Prince Albert was indeed a lover of Shakespeare, so our theory may be well founded. In any event Prince Albert's example should surely stir the hearts of all parents whose children are wrestling with *Macbeth* as an examination set book and encourage them to take a round trip to the wild landscape where events such as Shakespeare described actually happened more than a thousand years ago.

The days of genuine castles as places in which to live out a siege and launch periodic assaults on the enemy are over. Cawdor Castle, a few miles south-west of Nairn, is an example. Originally built in 1390, probably on the site of something simpler and cruder, it got altered over the years until, by 1650, its owner began to fit sash windows into the walls and turn it by degrees into one of Scotland's great houses. It still has a keep and a drawbridge and much of its fabric was probably part of the former castle, perhaps the one that belonged to Shakespeare's Thane, but it is no longer a defensive structure.

As if paying tribute to Scotland's unique history and tradition, one of our greatest Edwardian actors always wore two upturned Dundee cake tins fastened to his chain-mail across his chest when he performed Macbeth. I happen to know this because an old actress now long since deceased was his regular Lady Macbeth and often collided with them. And how appropriate that one of the most famous of British theatre companies should have planted itself in Pitlochry, the same magic ground.

The poet Byron sang of the isles of Greece 'where burning Sappho lived and sang'. But clinging to the west coast of Scotland lie the windswept inner Hebrides,

Between Speyside and Braemar are the magnificent Cairngorms, a worn-down granite upland, the remnant of a much higher range. How did that happen? you might ask. I sought help from my editor. 'Sit down, old chap,' he said, and I obeyed. 'Mountain ranges seem immovable, what you would call terra firma?' I agreed. 'But,' he said, 'more than one-eighth of an inch of the entire land surface is being worn away from beneath our feet every hundred years and highlands are planed down faster than lowlands.' 'How?' I asked. 'Wear and tear, like you and me,' he replied, 'only a lot slower. Only yesterday in geological time, glaciers were wearing away Scotland's mountains, and today frost splits rocks apart and rain washes the pieces downhill. These and other processes are unceasing, so imagine their effect over millions of years.' I promised to think about it. Now I've bought myself a book on geology.

crowned by Skye, with Rhum, Eigg, Coll, Tiree, Mull, Staffa, Colonsay, Jura and Islay hanging southwards like a precious necklace with tiny Iona, where St Columba landed in 563 and set to work to bring the savage Picts into the embrace of Christianity.

Lying in a long protective belt as if to guard the inner islands from the fury of the Atlantic gales lie a second string of islands, the Outer Hebrides: Lewis, Harris, North and South Uist, Eriskay and Barra. Here the water, the light, the hills, the ragged coastlines form a breath-taking assembly. These are indeed precious stones set in a silver sea. And beyond, even farther west is another girdle of protective rocks: Foula, Flannan, St Kilda, Fair Isle and Rockall. The Western Isles are a separate world. These are no ordinary Scots. They look different and speak a

Above: Highland Games are held at Braemar in September. At Highland Games, the great event – certainly the one most applauded by English folk – is tossing the caber, when strong men compete with each other to throw a tree trunk as far as possible. And then there are sword-fights, Highland dancing, with sandwiches and pies washed down with tea and whisky. Not so long ago and certainly well into the early 20th century, Britain also had the Cumberland Games and the Cotswold Games at which villagers showed off their skills and challenged neighbouring villages to compete with them. Cornish wrestlers even travelled to Cumberland to accept a challenge.

Above right: The Falls of Dochart are near Killin, which is near the south-western end of Loch Tay. Set amid some of Scotland's most superb scenery, this is an area for salmon and trout fishermen. You can imagine them standing in midstream, dressed in waders and mackintoshes, casting their flies into the boiling foam. An old poem reads:
'Enjoy thy stream, O gentle fish,
And when an angler for his dish,
Through gluttony's foul sin,
Attempts, the wretch, to pull thee out,
God give thee strength, O gentle trout,
To pull the rascal in'!

different tongue, clinging to soft Gaelic sounds and singing sweet Gaelic music.

It was at Eriskay in July 1745 that Bonnie Prince Charlie, accompanied by seven faithful followers, launched his ill-fated attempt to bring Great Britain back under Stuart rule. And it was here that we can imagine him hearing and even humming to himself some of the classic folk-songs of this remarkable sea-girt territory, such as the 'Eriskay Love Lilt', 'Land of Heart's Desire', 'Island Shieling Song', 'Kishmull's Galley', 'The Christchild's Lullaby', 'The Bens of Jura' and 'The Mull Fishers' Love Song'.

Little did he dream of the hazards that lay ahead, gathering a Highland army 3,000-strong, capturing Perth, Scotland's former capital and proclaiming his father king, then to Edinburgh's Holyroodhouse and Carlisle, gathering reinforcements on the way. Then the 300-mile (483-km) rearguard action winning brave but limited actions on the way until at last, in April 1746, he faced three times his own number at Culloden, one of the bloodiest battles in British history and saw his brave Highlanders crushed by the well-armed and well-trained English Redcoats under Bloody Cumberland – heirs of a magnificent army that had conquered half of Europe under Marlborough. Then came the five hazardous months getting back to the west coast and taking ship for France, never to return.

You can cover every inch of the ground and imagine every moment of that brave but fruitless adventure. It was a dream that turned into a nightmare. But behind their bravery and toughness and their superhuman competence, the Scots are inveterate dreamers and the land they inhabit is itself a land of dreams.

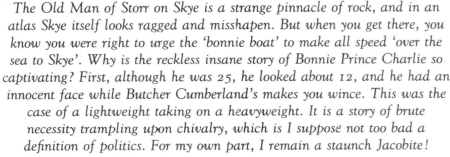

The Old Man of Storr on Skye is a strange pinnacle of rock, and in an atlas Skye itself looks ragged and misshapen. But when you get there, you know you were right to urge the 'bonnie boat' to make all speed 'over the sea to Skye'. Why is the reckless insane story of Bonnie Prince Charlie so captivating? First, although he was 25, he looked about 12, and he had an innocent face while Butcher Cumberland's makes you wince. This was the case of a lightweight taking on a heavyweight. It is a story of brute necessity trampling upon chivalry, which is I suppose not too bad a definition of politics. For my own part, I remain a staunch Jacobite!

Portree, on Skye, is tucked away safely on the west side of its own little sea loch. It is a pleasant headquarters for exploring the island, which is large — 50 miles (80 km) or so from stem to stern — and all of breathtaking beauty, with no spot more than 6 miles (10 km) from the sea. One of the most overwhelming sights is the Cuillin Hills in the south, while at Dunvegan Castle you can see a lock of Bonnie Prince Charlie's hair, a famous four-pint drinking horn and the Fairy Flag which guaranteed victory in battle, success in begetting an heir, and shoals of herring running into the loch whenever required.

237

The first time I was in Dublin, I crossed the O'Connell Bridge, shown here, and went to see some of the wonders of Irish antiquity – the Cross of Cong, the Tara Brooch, the Ardagh Chalice and the Book of Kells – and then on to a museum full of relics of the 1916 and 1919–21 Rebellions. A friend of ours in Essex owns a tattered pass, printed in English and Irish, which had been used in 1916 by her father, a postman employed by the loyalist army. With it he carried rebel mail across no-man's land into the General Post Office where the rebels had barricaded themselves, then returned safely. Such is the lunacy of war. The powerful presence of Jonathan Swift, greatest of all masters of English prose, still pervades Dublin's St Patrick's Cathedral. We did a version of Gulliver's Travels at The Mermaid Theatre, designed by the lamented Sean Kenny, the greatest stage designer of my time.

Ireland

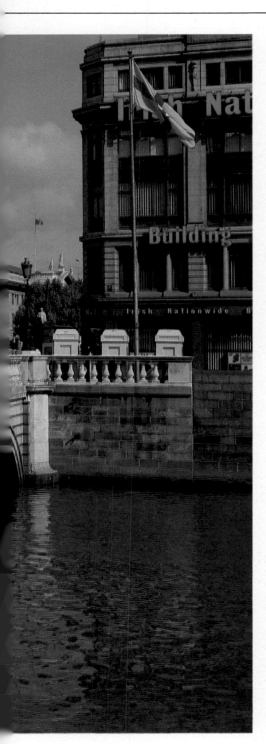

Across the Irish Sea from Great Britain lies Ireland, the other large island in the British Isles. Ireland was long known as 'the land of Saints and Scholars', and the index of the *Blue Guide to Ireland* contains the names of more than a hundred saints, from Aengus to Tigernach, and including such famous figures as Brendan, Columba, Kevin and Patrick. The Irish saints carried Christianity both to America and into the heart of Asia. One of the first Anglo-Irish songs my mother sang to me, at the age of four or five, went as follows:

'There's a dear little plant that grows in our
    Isle,
'Twas St Patrick himself sure that set it,
And the sun on his journey with pleasure did
    smile
And with dew from his eye often wet it.
And it shines through the bog, through break
    and the mireland,
And they call it the dear little shamrock of
    Ireland.
The dear little shamrock,
The sweet little shamrock,
The dear little, sweet little shamrock of
    Ireland.'

Some 40 years later, when I first visited Ireland accompanied by my old friend novelist and dramatist Bill Naughton, I suggested that we should go in search of early Christianity. First we went to Dublin, where archaeologists were digging up one of the largest Viking settlements west of Norway, and where the roots of Irish history are still being exposed. In the National Museum are many priceless relics of the early faith, including the delicate Tara Brooch, the silver Ardagh Chalice and the

Waterford is a manufacturing town famous for its glassware. It was founded by the Vikings, thereafter suffering repeated attacks by Anglo-Normans until 1650, when it surrendered to Oliver Cromwell on honourable terms. Its most dazzling relic is a set of medieval vestments, made around 1485 and discovered during the demolition of the Protestant Christchurch in 1773. It included copes, albs, tunics and dalmatics, everything made of rich brocaded velvet and cloth of gold with figure-embroidered orphreys of linen. On its discovery, it was presented by the Protestant bishop to the Roman Catholic one. The only matching display I have ever seen was one collected by Father Fynes Clinton, which he presented to the Church of St Magnus the Martyr in the City of London. Waterford was also the birthplace of the great comedienne Dorothy Jordan, mistress of the Duke of Clarence (later William IV) and mother of his numerous children. Charles Lamb said that her voice alone 'would melt a Methodist'.

Cross of Cong – all masterpieces of Christian art; while Trinity College Library contains the wondrous Book of Kells, a gloriously decorated version of the Gospels, written and painted in the 9th century and often described as the world's most beautiful book. Finally, at a performance of Sean O'Casey's *Juno and the Paycock* at Dublin's Abbey Theatre, we were able to relish the Anglo-Irish tongue in all its richness, and were reminded that the scholarly tradition in Ireland had been caught up and carried on by such great writers as Swift, Sheridan, Shaw, Wilde, Synge, Yeats, and Joyce, to name only a few.

From Dublin Bill and I headed south for Glendalough, one of Ireland's holiest places, chosen in the sixth century by Prince Kevin of Leinster as a refuge from the world and its lures. There, living a life of prayer and contemplation, he was joined by ever more disciples until Glendalough became a sort of Christian settlement, with

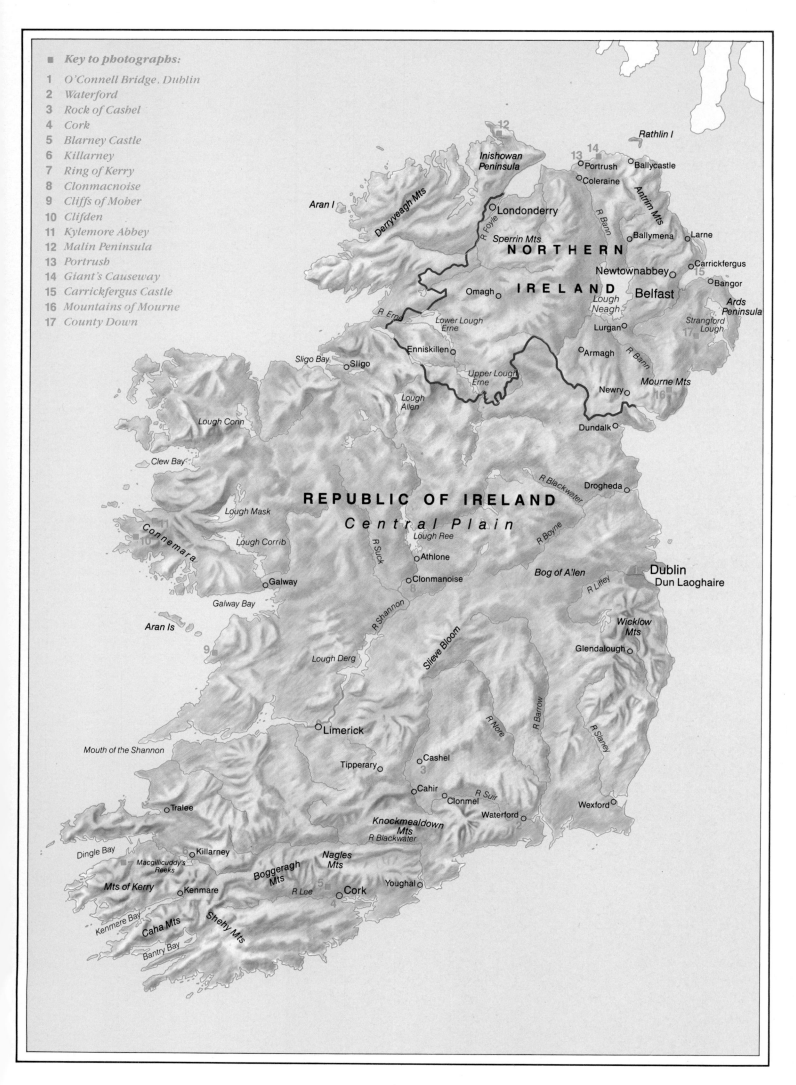

Key to photographs:

1 O'Connell Bridge, Dublin
2 Waterford
3 Rock of Cashel
4 Cork
5 Blarney Castle
6 Killarney
7 Ring of Kerry
8 Clonmacnoise
9 Cliffs of Moher
10 Clifden
11 Kylemore Abbey
12 Malin Peninsula
13 Portrush
14 Giant's Causeway
15 Carrickfergus Castle
16 Mountains of Mourne
17 County Down

its own tiny cathedral, a group of attendant churches and a watch-tower 100 feet (30 metres) high from which warnings were given when foes were approaching. The Normans later destroyed the settlement, but Kevin's name lives on as one of Ireland's greatest saints, and as a favourite Christian name for Irish boys.

From Glendalough we continued south to Wexford, which has dared to challenge such great centres as Glyndebourne and Salzburg with a yearly festival of music and drama; and, a short distance to the west, visited Waterford, world famous for its glassware. North-west of Waterford was Cashel, with its 300-foot (about 90-metre) high rock of solid limestone surmounted by the remains of a magnificent church sheltering Cormac's chapel, one of the jewels of Irish

Below left: The Rock of Cashel bears on its summit the ruins of the palace of the kings of Munster who ruled from the 4th to the beginning of the 12th century. The rock itself is a great limestone crag, 300 feet (91 metres) high, and the battered palace holds one of the jewels of Irish architecture, the tiny Chapel of Cormac. This was built by monks who had doubtless seen some genuine Romanesque architecture somewhere in Europe and who came home resolved to copy it. In fact their innocence helped them to outdo the original and someone has described it as an example of 'Eternity peeping through time'.

Bottom left: Blarney Castle is a ruin except for this impressive square keep, embodying the Blarney Stone, which endows the gift of persuasive speech on anyone who kisses it. It is said that Queen Elizabeth demanded that its owner Cormac McCarthy should acknowledge her sovereignty, but he procrastinated with such a stream of flattering and persuasive excuses that when she read his seventh letter written in the same honey-tongued Irish vein, she flew into a rage, crumpled the letter into a ball and threw it at the head of Sir Walter Raleigh, screaming: 'Don't give me any more of that blarney!' And that's how the word got fastened into the English language.

Right: Cork is a city I know and love, for I visited it every weekend during the six happy weeks I spent in Youghal in 1954, filming Moby Dick. It was once a British naval base and I heard of one delightful incident involving the fleet. When the first British company to tour Southern Ireland brought over the musical play Maritana in the late 1890s, there was silence at the first rehearsal. The first fiddle explained that none of the musicians could read music. They were accustomed to play only by ear and, unless the music was played to them on a piano, Maritana was out of the question. Finally, an SOS was sent off to the Commander of the British naval squadron. A band sent across to fill the gap scored a great success.

Top: Jaunting cars are familiar sights in Killarney. Ireland is renowned for a kind of incongruous humour, but its incongruity often contains a challenging degree of logic.

For example, a Cambridge scientist found himself at a railway station with a clock on both platforms, each telling a different time. He asked the station-master what was the good of two clocks if they told different times. The station-master replied: 'What would be the good of two clocks if they told the same time?' The jaunting car is a good example of this logic. Instead of passengers facing forwards seeing only the driver's back, or backwards seeing only the landscape long passed, or inwards, facing people for whom they may have little affection, they sit back to back against a central cushioned rail, facing outwards to enjoy the view. On the return journey, they enjoy the view they missed on the way out.

Above: The Ring of Kerry contains some of Ireland's loveliest landscapes. The whole area is also littered with the remains of early people: dolmens, ogamstones, chamber graves, beehive monasteries and early cross pillars with the Christian sign chi ro scratched on them. Here we really are in on the birth-throes of Christianity, where monks escaped from the heathen east to the land's end in the west. Jesus had promised: 'Yet a little while and I come again.' The end of the world was at hand. How best to prepare? The answer was easy. 'Watch and pray for ye know not when the time cometh.' How best to pray? 'Face to face with ourselves in tiny walled cells, shutting out everything, our fears but not our faith.' To the north, on the Dingle peninsula, is the tiny Gallarus Oratory which might shelter eight to ten souls from the blast. Compared with a cell, it was more like a cathedral.

architecture. This tiny structure suggests that its builders had once seen a Norman church, had done their best to remember what it was like and had outdone the original.

One of my happiest memories of southern Ireland came on another visit in the 1950s to the seaside village of Youghal, to the east of Cork. A flourishing port throughout the 18th and 19th centuries, it harboured the great three- and four-masters of the transatlantic traffic, But steam power gradually rendered Youghal super-fluous and it had fallen into disrepair until a film crew transformed it into the New Bedford from which, in Herman Melville's great story *Moby Dick*, the whale-ship *Pequod* sets sail on her ill-fated voyage. Suddenly and without warning, this village was hit by a hundred-odd members of the Association of Cine Technicians, the

Clonmacnoise, in County Offaly on the Shannon River, contains the treasured remnants of a tiny Christian settlement following more than 1,000 years of suffering at the hands of Vikings, English and fellow Irish. Here are parts of a cathedral surrounded by six tiny attendant churches, like bridesmaids, inside a walled park, complete with graveyard. Its slabs of raw stone are scratched with the names of the dead in Gaelic beneath rudely inscribed crosses. There were once six or seven other churches and a village full of people. But Clonmacnoise still has one of Ireland's finest round towers, with its only entrance 15 feet (4.6 metres) from the ground.

The Cliffs of Moher, in County Clare, offer stout resistance against the punishment handed out by the Atlantic waves. Elsewhere in the British Isles, especially in parts of eastern England, the sea is winning and whole villages have disappeared over the years, although in places the coast is being built up by sand and shingle or is advancing as the sea retreats, leaving villages stranded far inland, as at Formby in Lancashire. The Moher Cliffs are 600 feet (183 metres) high and built of shales, sandstones and flagstones. But even higher cliffs can be seen on the lonely bird sanctuary of Rockall, 240 miles (386 km) west of the Outer Hebrides.

National Association of Theatrical and Kinematograph Employees, the Electrical Trade Union and British Actors' Equity, led by the fabled director John Huston. Here we lived and worked for five lyrical weeks, recreating all the preliminaries of the *Pequod*'s departure for the great hunt.

While making the film, Bert Lloyd, who was playing the *Pequod*'s leading shantyman, made a pilgrimage to Kerry to meet one of the last traditional Irish story-tellers, who would visit people's homes and entertain them with folk tales lasting several hours. Bert heard the story of a boy who left home and had a string of hair-raising adventures before getting back again. Such stories were often as complex as Homer's *Odyssey*, full of twists and turns of great humour and inventiveness. In the old days, when books were rare in villages and isolated homesteads, story-telling was an important feature of life, especially at birthdays, weddings and funerals.

On free days, I visited Killarney and its lovely lakes, rode on a jaunting car in which two rows of passengers sit (very sensibly) back to back along a central bar, facing outwards in order to enjoy the scenery. On a longer trip, I saw Ireland's highest mountain range, Macgillicuddy's Reeks, and went around the celebrated scenic route

At pony shows like this one at Clifden, Connemara, the Irish are always ready to do a little horse-trading, even on Sundays, as shown by a story taken from James Lloyd's charming little book My Circus Life: 'On the road I met a gentleman riding a beautiful red and white horse. I stopped him, and asked if he would sell it. He replied: "Supposing it was not Sunday, I would." I said: "Supposing it was not Sunday, what do you ask for the horse?" "Supposing it was not Sunday, I would take £35." I said: "Now supposing it was not Sunday, I will give you £28." He said: "My last word. If it was not Sunday I would take £30." I said: "Supposing it was not Sunday, I will give you that sum." "Right, let's suppose it's not Sunday," he replied. I agreed, bought the horse and named it "Supposition".' I would guess that there's not a man who wouldn't do otherwise.

247

Kylemore Abbey, Connemara, is a large castle-like folly built by a rich Liverpool businessman in 1866. Following the owner's death, it became the headquarters of the Dames Irlandaise from Ypres, France, whose convent had been destroyed by shellfire in 1914, and thus it has continued. The sisters are a teaching branch of the Benedictine Order. One of them founded a pottery at the abbey and this is now a flourishing concern.

known as the Ring of Kerry. I also saw fishermen using the traditional Irish curraghs, made of cowhide stretched over a bowl-shaped framework of ash then coated with hot tar for waterproofing, some of the tiny beehive cells in which early monks lived, and, on the Dingle peninsula, the Gallarus Oratory, a dry-stone chapel dating back to the Dark Ages, whose roof resembles an upturned boat. One of the loveliest of my journeys from Youghal was to Thurles, in Tipperary, then through Roscrea, with its magnificent ruined priory, and on to Birr and Cong,

Five Fingers Beach is near Malin, Donegal. Here shallow waves crawl slowly up the foreshore, the force of the incoming sea having been checked on the rocks farther out. Malin Head is the northernmost tip of western Ireland, although the tiny island of Inishrahull 4 miles (6 km) beyond give a hint of the passion which drove early Christians to seek the loneliest places for prayer and contemplation. Here were discovered a few foundation stones and an ancient cross owned by the hermit who long ago had found solace and strength in this final patch of God's green earth. After the comparative regularity of the north coast of Sligo and Donegal Bay, the whole 90-mile (145-km) stretch northwards is wild and rocky, backed by mountains, inhospitable and scantily populated, but recklessly beautiful.

between Loughs Corrib and Mask. The Cross of Cong in the National Museum comes from Cong's beautiful ruined abbey.

I also visited Clonmacnoise, County Offaly, whose cathedral is one of the marvels of early Christianity. It was founded by St Kieron in AD 548, when Irish masons were not yet able to cope with the scale of building we associate with the word cathedral. Instead, they did something more impressive. They built as big a one as they could manage with six tiny churches clustered

Portrush, the playground of Northern Ireland and one of its finest seaside resorts, stands on a promontory and offers high-quality fishing, golfing, swimming and other delights. It is at the western end of the Antrim Coast and Glens Area of Outstanding Natural Beauty, which includes the Giant's Causeway, and it provides regular excursions to this unique demonstration of the work of nature.

Right: According to legend, the Giant's Causeway in County Antrim was built by an Irish giant, Finn MacCool, to link Ireland and Scotland, and for a long time the volcanic origin of the causeway was not understood. In 1694 a speaker at the Royal Society said in all seriousness that the causeway could not be man-made because there was no mortar between the columns!

Below: Carrickfergus Castle, planted on a rocky spur above Belfast harbour, is one of Ireland's finest surviving castles. I have pointed out how Yorkshire, Wales and the Western Isles of Scotland were littered with castles and how, all too often, they fell far short of defensive capability and how easily they seem to have got knocked down. I also believe that Caernarfon, built in 1283, is the last word in the art of castle-building. But Carrickfergus, built in 1180, two centuries before Edward I, looks like a true forerunner in this vital art.

around it, together with a watch-tower as fine as the one at Glendalough. They also erected roughly carved gravestones above the bodies of their dead. At Clonmacnoise, even more intensely than at Essex's Bradwell on Sea, Christianity shines forth in its primal colours. Here, if anywhere in Europe, you will shed tears and say your prayers.

To the west at Clifden, Connemara, you can see one of the propellor blades of the Vicker's Vimy biplane which carried Alcock and Whitten-Brown from Newfoundland to Ireland in the first transatlantic flight (1919). North of Clifden is the lovely Achill Island, County Mayo, which boasts some of Ireland's most spectacular cliffs.

Northern Ireland has not only historic cities and towns, such as Londonderry, but also seven Areas of Outstanding Natural Beauty. Perhaps the best known of these is the Antrim Coast and Glens, between Larne and Portrush. The highlight here is the spectacular Giant's Causeway, whose six-sided basalt columns are complemented by others in Scotland. North-east of Londonderry, around Magilligan's Point, which almost

The Mountains of Mourne, County Down, remind me that a lullaby sung to me by my mother asserted that she was 'longing to be where the Mountains of Mourne sweep down to the sea'. She told me that these mountains were in Ireland and that Ireland was a beautiful country. I also remember my father claiming that 'When Irish eyes are smiling . . . you can hear the angels sing.' This seemed an exaggeration, but as a dutiful boy I did not venture to question it. Recently I came across an old book entitled Irish Songs and Ballads, *containing 42 items of which I recalled 16. A third of the songs were written or composed by Irishmen. I suppose they were part of an attempt to make amends for the many cruelties inflicted by England on the Emerald Isle, and to convince the English that Ireland was, as I can attest, even more beautiful than these songs made it out to be.*

251

I have written in this book of castles and abbeys, of bridges, aircraft, ships, motor cars, roads and railways, of battles and sieges, of great houses and holiday camps, of mountains, lochs and rivers, of the underlying structures and formations on which Britain is planted, almost forgetting that the greatest achievement of the people of the British Isles is to have found a land almost completely covered by dense forest and, over the centuries, to have beaten it, nursed it and wooed it into the world's greatest farming country. George III was known affectionately as 'Farmer George' and the British and Irish are, without realizing it, his spiritual progeny. Think of Kent, the Vale of Aylesbury, Hereford and Worcester, Rutland, Devonshire, the Borders and, here in this picture, County Down. We could almost interchange their photographs, certainly without giving offence, because this is something of which we can be eternally proud and which goes to the very root of our being.

cuts Lough Foyle off from the sea, are superb beaches, lonely dunes and mud-flats. South of Londonderry are the Sperrin Mountains, a wilderness with sparkling rivers and standing stones erected in prehistoric times. Not far from Belfast are the tranquil Lagan Valley and Strangford Lough, a huge inlet of the sea with only the narrowest of outlets; and in the south-eastern corner of Northern Ireland are the famed Mountains of Mourne whose highest point, Slieve Donard, 'sweeps down to the sea'.

One of my most cherished memories of Ireland is of a visit made by the Old Vic Company to Belfast Opera House in 1948 with a production of *The Taming of the Shrew*, in which Trevor Howard gave the most captivating performance of Petruchio I have ever seen. On the closing night of the two-week season, a large crowd assembled outside the stage door to cheer the company off to the docks. A week or so later, I received a letter with a Belfast postmark asking me for an autographed photograph. The writer said: 'I was in the crowd which saw you all off at the end of your season at the Opera House. I was the girl who had just had her hair permed.' What a tribute! What an honour!

Index

Figures in italic type refer to illustrations

Place names only are indexed
Abbreviations used:
   D. & G. for Dumfries and Galloway
   H. & W. for Hereford and Worcester
   H'land for Highland (Scotland)
   S'clyde for Strathclyde (Scotland)